W0010516

WIRED

# WIRED

## CONTEMPORARY ZULU TELEPHONE-WIRE BASKETS

by David Arment and Marisa Fick-Jordaan
photographs by Andrew Cerino

published by S/C EDITIONS · SANTA FE

distributed by MUSEUM OF NEW MEXICO PRESS · SANTA FE

distributed in Africa by DAVID KRUT PUBLISHING · JOHANNESBURG

## ACKNOWLEDGMENTS

*To Jim, for taking me on my first trip to Africa, which changed our lives,*
*and for helping me find a way to turn a good idea into reality;*
*and to Trisha, for her passion for Africa and for her support—it can be done!*
—David Arment

*To Jan and Jan-Paul, and for Margaret Daniel, who has helped all the way.*
—Marisa Fick-Jordaan

This book was made possible by the generous
support of the Wilson Education Foundation.

*The Wilson Education Foundation (WEF) was set up to endow financially*
*disadvantaged high school graduates in the United States with*
*four-year college scholarships, as well as to provide scholarships and*
*other educational or medical assistance to organizations worldwide.*
*The WEF is currently funding specific initiatives to improve schools in rural South Africa.*
*The WEF has also become involved in the fight against AIDS, and the administration*
*of care and support to children whose lives are affected by AIDS.*
*More information about the WEF can be found at www.wilsoneducationfoundation.org.*

Proceeds from the sale of this book benefit the Wilson Education Foundation.

previous pages, left:

**BLACK-AND-WHITE PLATE WITH INITIALS E. M.**
Elliot Mkhize
324 x 290 mm
Collection of David Arment

opposite page:

**BHEKI SIBIYA DEMONSTRATING THE HARD-WIRE WEAVING TECHNIQUE**
Photographed at the BAT Centre
January 2004

# CONTENTS

**THIS BOOK WOULD NOT HAVE BEEN POSSIBLE
WITHOUT THE GENEROUS SPONSORSHIP OF:**

Doug & Lisa Allen

Bartel Arts Trust

Bergamo Fabrics

Barbara Buzzell

Lynn Caldwell

Susan & Vance Campbell

Melissa M. Carry, M.D., P.A.

Casa Nova

Todd Davis & Chris Richter

Natalie Fitz-Gerald

Susan & Charles Fradin

Carolyn Franklin & Roger Polan

Thelma Glassman

Marcella M. McDaneld

Emily & Herman Mauney

George & Christie Mazuera

Curtis B. Medford & Trikes
    Wallcovering Source

In memory of Pete & Micky Pedersen

Jim Rimelspach

Beth, Bob, Lindsey, & Lauren Sawyer

Kelly & Carol Trimmer

Susan Tonjes

Joan Warren & Steve Grady

Trisha Wilson

Wilson and Associates

previous pages, left:
**HARD-WIRE BOWL**
Alice Gcaba
120 × 380 mm

opposite page, clockwise from top left:
**SOFT-WIRE BOWL**
Joseph Msomi
190 mm diameter, Private Collection
**SOFT-WIRE BOWL**
Artist unknown
165 mm diameter, Private Collection
**SOFT-WIRE BOWL**
Joseph Msomi
190 mm diameter, Private Collection
**SOFT-WIRE BOWL**
Artist unknown
180 mm diameter, Private Collection

# WHY THE WIRE PLATES?

At its heart, this book tells a story, which is long overdue, about the traditions and resourcefulness of a group of Zulu weavers and the individuals who helped turn a craft into fine art. The objects of this art form—the baskets, sticks, bottles, and other wire pieces—are a collector's dream. Traveling through South Africa on the safari circuit, one has time for a stopover in the cities, Johannesburg, Cape Town, and Durban, to do some shopping. The attraction of these beautiful objects is clear, and they are to be found in many an overweight bag checked in for flights back to the United States or Europe.

A photograph in a brochure for tourists was my first exposure to telephone-wire baskets. Colorful and distinctive, they stood out from the typical tourist curios of carved giraffes and beaded jewelry. This was during the early 1990s, and the few baskets that were available had designs of simple zigzags and swirls. The colors were basic, and the wire was in many cases truly recycled from scrap dealers and the local telephone lines. The quest began.

I started collecting baskets—when I could find them—on annual trips to South Africa. I began to seek out sources and to follow the development of the art. Soon I noticed that

opposite page:

**WHY THE WIRE PLATES?**
Bheki Dlamini
345 mm diameter
Collection of Paul Mikula

1

simple figures started showing up in the baskets. Letters and words were integrated into the work and the color and design became more complex and artistic. My passion became intense, and I found myself tracking down baskets from New York to Paris, and broadening my collection to include other quirky and historic Zulu wire objects. Little did I know at the time that my personal interest was so closely aligned with the development of the baskets into an art form and the beginning of an international marketing effort by the BAT Shop (an arts and crafts development center) in Durban. While I was busy collecting, Marisa Fick-Jordaan was, unbeknownst to me, working with the weavers of Siyanda (a residential area outside Durban), helping to turn an rural craft into an art form and supplying baskets to Art Africa and other shops. Sharing a passion for telephone-wire baskets, we needed only to connect.

A close mutual friend, Marianne Fassler, the icon of South African fashion, brought us together. We visited Siyanda together; a hot awakening for a Texan used to high rises and air-conditioned everything. Then, on a steamy evening in Durban after an exceptional day, we plotted this book over whisky prawns.

There was very little formal documentation on the baskets and we knew that a book on telephone wire had to be written. We had our storytellers, Marisa herself and Paul Mikula, who were there in the beginning, encouraging and promoting. Karel Nel, associate professor of fine art at the University of the Witwatersrand, while battling malaria, agreed to write the foreword in order to provide some context for the baskets and to explain their connection to the development of wire-working in southern Africa. The baskets and objects spoke for themselves and we gained access to collections in South Africa as well as in the United States.

But the process is only a minor part of the story. This book is about the development of the craft, about the weavers, the Siyanda community, the collectors, and the beautiful works of art. This book is about how a group of people came together, elevating a rural craft to a new and exciting urban art form that has acquired well-deserved international recognition and acclaim.

—David Arment

opposite page:
**YELLOW BOWL WITH FIGURES**
Zodwa Maphumulo
470 mm diameter
Collection of David Arment

# RE-WIRED

Transformations of the wire-working traditions in the southern African region

by Karel Nel

Within the southern African context, wire has for eons been associated with the manufacture and embellishment of high-status objects. During our own time wire has, to a large degree, lost its value or specialness and is taken much for granted. But this was not always so. The skills required for drawing wire in Africa were both highly complex and extraordinarily labor-intensive, which meant that a piece of wire was, traditionally, a rare and expensive commodity. Early examples of wire as a valuable trade item are to be found in the currencies produced in the Cross River region of Nigeria from the sixteenth through the eighteenth centuries: these short lengths of drawn wire were bundled and traditionally bound and bent into a U shape. They were often found at archeological sites, and are associated specifically with burials.

In southern Africa, too, wire, often in the form of tightly wound anklets and bracelets, is found in archeological sites, once again mainly in association with burials. An opulent use of drawn copper and brass is to be found in the woven wire-work that embellished important personal objects during the nineteenth and early twentieth centuries, particularly among Zulu speakers and other, related, Nguni groups. For example, small gourd snuff containers

opposite page:
**CARVED WOOD HAT WITH WIRE DETAILS**
From the H. C. Lugg Collection
Signed "Hat carved from the root of a umkhuhlu tree by a
native of Kosi Bay . . . purchased by me . . . in 1920, H. C. Lugg"
330 x 265 x 900 mm
Campbell Collections, Durban

were frequently decorated with brass and copper wire in refined, geometric patterns, an indication of the social significance of these small objects and of their association with the *amadlozi* (ancestral spirits).

Copper and brass were highly valued commodities throughout Africa—and southern Africa was no exception. Here, particularly in the Zulu court, Shaka, Dingaan, and a succession of leaders centralized and controlled access to the metal. This meant that the metals were used for high-status objects associated with centralized power, among them the *ingxotha,* the brass cuff-like ornaments awarded for bravery, and the heavy brass beads known as *ndondo,* worn only by those held in high esteem in the kingdom. Finely woven wire was used to decorate significant objects, such as staffs of office and ceremonial batons, particularly during the period of the great military might of Shaka and the Zulu empire. Many fine examples of objects adorned in this manner were collected during the Anglo-Zulu Wars and taken back to Britain. In recent years considerable numbers of these artifacts have been brought back to and are now included in important public collections such as those of the Johannesburg Art Gallery, the Standard Bank Collection of African Art at the University of the Witwatersrand, the Durban Art Gallery, the National Gallery in Cape Town, and the Campbell Collections in Durban.

A major aesthetic revolution occurred in Nguni culture when small, brightly colored glass beads were introduced by early European traders and missionaries. These beads, manufactured in Bohemia, were imported in large quantities for trade and barter. They, like the metals, were largely controlled by the ruling power, at least until the mid-1850s, when the royal monopolies started to wane. The introduction of the beads led to the development of a complex visual language within the beadwork, signaling group identity, social and marital status, and other nuanced information—all through the evolution of intricate geometric patterns and specific color sequences.

These beads inevitably found their way onto the traditional *izimbenge* (baskets used as pot lids). The pots in which traditional beer was brewed were closely associated with the ancestral realm and so, by association, were the *izimbenge,* which kept dust from the beer and protected this sacred substance. It is therefore not surprising that these baskets were embellished with the precious beads, an indication of their importance and of their ritual connection with the *amadlozi.*

In time, this complex visual language would form the basis of the patterns that emerged in the new wire-basket tradition, which developed in the 1980s as the *imbenge* (a single

opposite page, clockwise from top left:

**THREE GOURDS WITH COPPER-WIRE DETAIL**
Artist unknown
Early 20th century
h: 175, 87, and 53 mm
Collection of the Phansi Museum, Durban

**WOODEN STICK WITH BRASS-WIRE DETAIL**
Artist unknown
Late 19th or early 20th century
h: 765 mm
Collection of David Arment

**IVORY SNUFF BOTTLES WITH COPPER WIRE**
Artist unknown
Early 20th century
h: 101 and 115 mm
Collection of the Phansi Museum, Durban

**SET OF HEAVY NDONDO BRASS BEADS OF HIGH STATUS**
Artist unknown
19th century
Zulu, Southern Africa
Collection of the Standard Bank Collection
of African Art, Johannesburg

**THREE GOURDS COVERED IN WIRE**
Artist unknown
20th century
h: 62, 85, and 77 mm
Collection of the Phansi Museum, Durban

basket) and its associated beadwork played a pivotal role in the evolution of the craft. The use of telephone wire for *izimbenge* locked together three traditions in a new syntax (see images page 18). Firstly, the copper wire, the high-status commodity used to embellish traditionally important objects, had become a valuable substitute for grass in the great basket-making tradition, shifting the very nature of the object itself. Secondly, the traditional form of the *imbenge* was adopted initially for the new baskets, which only later became considerably larger and shallower (hence their description as "plates")—or, at times, deeper. Thirdly, the colored, plastic sheathing of the wire introduced a wide variety of colors into the equation, displacing the traditional bead embellishment and resulting in rich, regularly textured surfaces with numerous chromatic shifts. The complex, geometric patterns that evolved in the new wire baskets have their ancestry in traditional patterns, but require of the weavers an understanding of the mathematics inherent in those patterns.

There was traditionally a strong, gendered relationship in Zulu culture to both the manufacture and use of specific objects: wood carving and metal forging or casting were very much part of the male domain; working with clay, in the making of pots, and intricate beadwork were traditionally part of the female domain. Basket weaving is an interesting anomaly; it seems to have been practiced by both men and women and the custom is still followed in the weaving of wire baskets. Weaving with copper wire might be expected to fall, if loosely, into the male domain of metal working; the complex colored syntax of woven patterns might be expected to be associated with the female domain of beadwork.

Most traditional items were produced for a specific use within a prescribed cultural context and often bore strong ritual overtones that were deeply embedded in the matrix of the culture. The Nguni cultures of southern Africa were by and large nomadic, with cattle central to both the culture and its economy. The cattle were at the very heart of perceptions of self-worth, the means of social reciprocity, the sacred link to the ancestral world, the *amadlozi,* and were above all, a barometer of social order and stability. The nomadic life style associated with cattle keeping meant that personal possessions were necessarily few. Such objects as were made and kept would, also necessarily, be small and useful—a headrest, a milk pail, a meat platter, pots, *izimbenge* and other baskets, small snuff containers, beadwork, and ceremonial sticks. These few items, though, were of great significance. They were made with great attention to both form and detail and sometimes were embellished with particular care. In a nomadic culture there is no place for the grand pieces of furniture, large paintings, bronzes, or other artifacts of this order that are generally considered by Westerners as art.

The objects, by nature small, domestic, and personal, rather than large, public, and institutional, were therefore almost invisible to most Westerners as legitimate expressions of artistic impulse and, consequently, were relegated to the status of mere craft or cultural artifact; the region was understood to have produced no art. This colonial attitude persisted and has changed only slowly despite serious studies of the complex value systems underpinning seemingly everyday objects. Nonetheless, consolidated private and public collections have helped to create a body of material that now allows people to compare and contrast works and to begin to recognize a gestalt for the southern African work.

These opportunities have produced a change in the assessment of the objects, with the collections migrating from ethnographic museums to art museums and a concomitant shift in the perceptions of scholars and the public. This reevaluation, and the understanding that there is, indeed, a southern African aesthetic, has lead to a renewed interest in the objects, with the work being regarded less as craft and more as art. Traditional nineteenth-century southern African pieces now change hands for astronomical sums in the major auction houses in New York and Paris.

That this new appreciation has clearly had an effect on contemporary production is to be seen in this sumptuous publication. As new markets opened up for early traditional pieces, so too a market has opened for the contemporary. In the past, pieces produced specifically for the Western market were curios, that is objects that no longer had any purpose within the context of traditional ritual, but were strategically adapted to the demands of another market and a different aesthetic. The fact that the objects were being produced for a new market altered their form, function, and aesthetic. The same kinds of changes are apparent in the evolution of the modern wire basket.

We see in this publication that, where distinctive objects of high quality are produced within a broad framing context, the function and symbolic significance of the *izimbenge* have largely evaporated; new demands and changing functions have altered the form and aesthetic of the baskets. This change is mirrored in the *imbenge* itself. No longer the traditional small bowl, of which the convex, upper surface was the more important and most finely decorated, the contemporary *izimbenge* have wide, flared bowls and flattened platter-like forms, with decorated interior, concave surfaces. They have become more like roundels or flat works that may easily be hung on walls. Losing their traditional functionality entirely, they have become more like paintings as they have been adapted for the Western fine-art market.

**TWO ALUMINUM WIRE BRACELETS**
Artist unknown
20th Century
60 x 60 and 145 x 80 mm
Collection of the Phansi Museum, Durban

9

These shifts have come about only after many years of mentoring and encouragement by an array of dedicated individuals who have been passionate about ensuring that this rich tradition and extraordinary skill continue to thrive, and who have made it possible for the weavers to develop their skills to create these remarkable objects and to make a living. The evolution of these changes is chronicled, both visually and verbally, in this publication. The nurturing guidance of some of the people who are part of this evolution is legendary and I cherish the memories of those whom I have had contact with or met over the years, particularly Jo Thorpe of the African Art Centre in Durban, Tessa Katzenellembogen and Creina Alcock, whose early encouragement laid the foundation of much of what was to come, Marisa Fick-Jordaan of the BAT Centre, whose innovation and steadfastness have carried a tide of talent into the new century. The establishment of the FNB Vita Craft Now awards—by which outstanding practitioners of the art have been encouraged and singled out, among them Elliot Mkhize, Ntombifuthi Magwasa, Zama Khanyile, and Vincent Sithole—has affirmed the importance of their work locally, nationally, and internationally.

This book celebrates the efflorescence of skill and creativity associated with wire work. It focuses on the innate ability of traditional artists and craftspeople to reinvent their skills and aesthetics in response to the introduction of new materials, adapting and developing them to their own ends and creating an astoundingly innovative beauty, addressing tradition and change, and literally reinventing the past.

opposite page, clockwise from top left:

**COPPER BOWL WITH PEARL BEADS**
Artist unknown
178 mm diameter
Collection of David Arment

**COPPER WIRE OVER ALUMINUM-WIRE BOWL**
Thulani Ngubane
241 mm diameter
Private Collection

**COPPER-WIRE BOWL**
Elias Mshengu
336 mm diameter
Private Collection

**"WOVEN" COPPER-WIRE PLATE**
Lindelani Ngwenya
336 mm diameter
Collection of David Arment

# SONG OF PRAISE

by Paul Mikula

In traditional Nguni society, all newcomers are introduced
or introduce themselves by describing their origins,
their families, their achievements, and their circumstances.

Important people have their own praise singers to do this for them.

Let us sing the praises of these baskets, which nowadays they call plates,
so that everyone will be familiar with their background and history.

*These are wire baskets—telephone-wire baskets—made by the Nguni people*
*to sell to the* abalungu *(white people) and* abafunduki *(foreigners).*
*Recently our own people have started to buy them as presents for visitors.*

*They call these baskets art, although we do not have a word in our vocabulary for "art."*
*We do have many words for "beauty" and for how well things are made. We use those*
*words for these baskets: they are absolutely beautiful and extremely well made. One*
*needs only to hold one to appreciate it. They are made from the fine telephone wires*

opposite page:
**CLAY ZULU BEER POTS WITH TELEPHONE-WIRE** *IZIMBENGE*
Artists unknown
20th century
Beer Pots: Collection of the Phansi Museum, Durban
*Izimbenge*: Collections of David Arment, Marisa Fick-Jordaan,
and the Phansi Museum, Durban

13

that are found inside larger plastic- or rubber-sheathed cables,

which we used to get from scrap-metal merchants or

from our friends who worked on telephone installations.

We call the wire scoobie wire.

In making the baskets, one is limited to the ten colors normally found

in the large cables: white, brown, green, yellow, gray, pink, blue, red,

black, and purple. In addition there are wires of those same colors

and either a horizontal stripe or a ring coding, so that there is an even bigger choice for

the installation engineer and for the basket maker.

In the old days a basket maker, usually a Zulu-speaking night watchman

with time on his hands, would hunt down a piece of cable

and then produce his objects in ever duller colors,

until he had used up even the most unexciting colors,

the striped and banded and brown wires generally coming last.

The telephone wire itself is made up of a thin plastic skin over single copper core. This

makes it extremely strong and so may be pulled tight when woven into the basket. These

scoobie wires, originally covered in rubber and subsequently in

PVC (polyvinyl chloride), have been available in South Africa since the 1930s,

although we really only started using them for baskets in the 1950s.

One still sees many old telephone-wire objects about, such as walking sticks banded with

wire or bottles covered from head to toe

in beautifully woven scoobie-wire dresses.

Because organic pigments were used in the older wires, the colors

were sensitive to ultraviolet light. They quickly became bleached out and the

coating became brittle. Later, inorganic, mineral-based pigments were used;

the colors lasted longer and the coating remained flexible.

It is easy to see which piece is new and which is old,

unless an old item has been hidden in the dark corner of a

kist (wooden chest), just to fool some innocent research student.

Some artists today no longer use telephone wire at all, preferring to

use panel wire because it is even thinner and has a diameter of only 0.22 mm.

Some makers even have wire especially made for them.

No more looking for scraps and making baskets from whatever could be found, no sir!

Many of today's artists specify the colors and the thicknesses of their materials.

opposite page:
**THREE TELEPHONE-WIRE PLATES**
Artists unknown
310 mm diameter, Collection of the Phansi Museum, Durban
330 mm diameter, Campbell Collections, Durban
260 mm diameter, Collection of the Phansi Museum, Durban

*Isn't that wonderful!*

*The telephone wire is only a part of the basket.*
*The structure of a basket is based on a spiral of thick wire around which*
*the thinner telephone wire is wound and held together with tight loops*
*also of telephone wire. This is what we call the hard-wire technique.*
*This particular technique is as old as grass basket making itself; wire has been*
*substituted for the various grasses of the core and the palm leaves used for binding.*

*There is another, more complex way of making a bowl: the soft-wire technique,*
*which is based on the traditional method of covering walking sticks and snuff*
*containers with various metal wires, a method that is still used*
*for covering walking and traditional dancing sticks and bottles.*
*A cover of telephone wire is plaited (braided) over a bowl- or plate-shaped object,*
*and then the mold is removed. Objects made according to this method*
*do not have the inherent strength of those made with a heavy-wire core,*
*but the technique produces marvelous diagonal designs,*
*although the variety is limited, and a much lighter product.*
*In these days of air freight and international tourists,*
*that has become an important consideration.*

*Because the technique based on a structural core permits a great variety of designs,*
*it is unlikely to be supplanted. The core wire used today is generally made of*
*galvanized mild steel and ranges from approximately 0.6 through 1.2 mm in diameter.*
*Available in rolls at hardware stores, it is easy to bend and holds its shape well.*
*Before the 1960s, the core wire used was generally 19 S.W.G. (standard wire gauge) ordi-*
*nary mild steel wires, which turn black with age and eventually rust away.*

*Wire weaving as a craft was first used for walking sticks and bottles,*
*but the true ancestor of wire weaving as an art is the* imbenge, *the beer pot lid.*
*Traditionally this lid, woven of grass and palm leaf,*
*is one of the most important household objects in the Zulu homestead*
*because it covers the* ukhamba *(clay beer pot).*
*It allows the beer to breathe and prevents dive-bombing kamikaze insects*
*from intoxicating and possibly obliterating themselves in the beverage.*

*Among the Nguni people the drinking of beer is a quasi-sacred event because*
*it is done to honor the* amadlozi *(ancestral spirits), who are themselves not*
*averse to partaking in the celebrations and for whom a special little pot is set*

opposite page, clockwise from top left:
**TELEPHONE WIRE OVER WOOD STICKS**
Artists unknown
Top, h: 1080 mm, Collection of Marisa Fick-Jordaan
Center, h: 1030 mm, Collection of the Phansi Museum, Durban
Bottom, h: 950 mm, Collection of Marisa Fick-Jordaan

**TELEPHONE WIRE OVER WOOD STICKS**
Artists unknown
Top, h: 670 mm, Collection of the Phansi Museum, Durban
Center, h: 990 mm, Collection of the Phansi Museum, Durban
Bottom, h: 690 mm, Collection of the Phansi Museum, Durban

**TELEPHONE WIRE OVER WOOD STICKS**
Artists unknown
Top, h: 550 mm, Collection of the Phansi Museum, Durban
Center, h: 990 mm, Collection of the Phansi Museum, Durban
Bottom, h: 800 mm, Collection of Marisa Fick-Jordaan

**SANGOMA SWISH WITH TELEPHONE-WIRE-COVERED HANDLE**
20th century
h: 700 mm, Collection of Marisa Fick-Jordaan

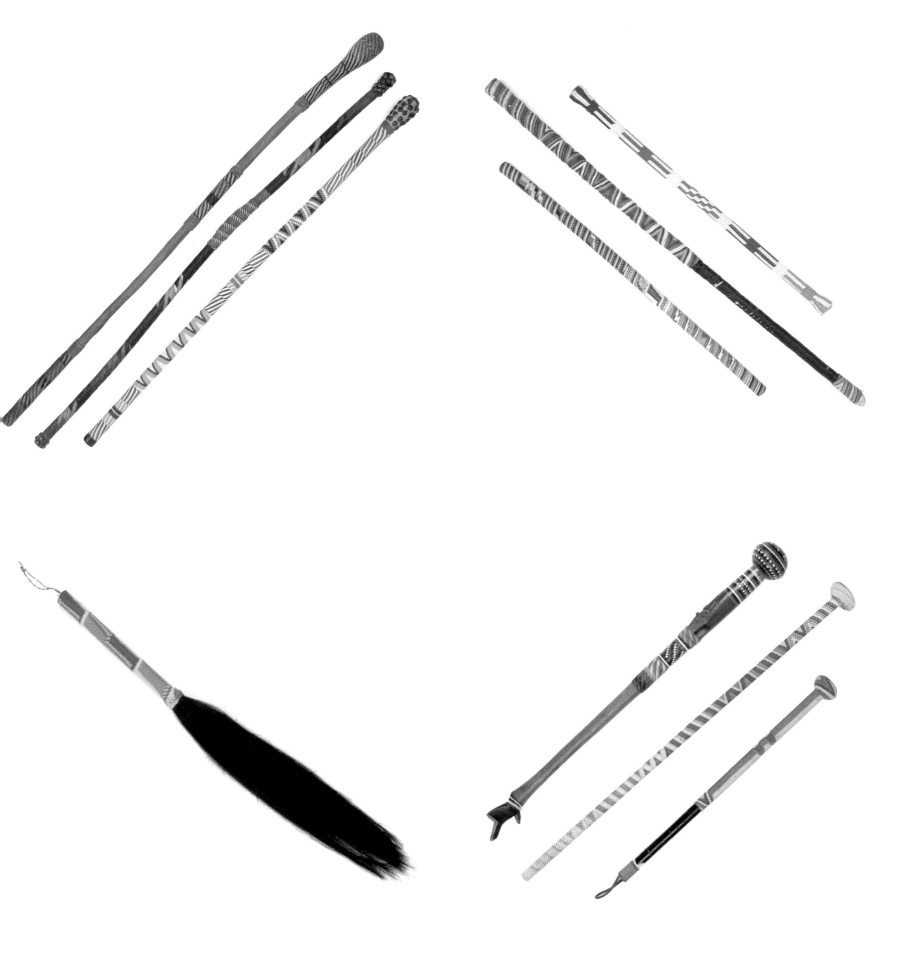

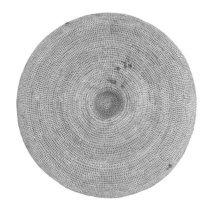
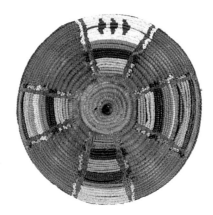

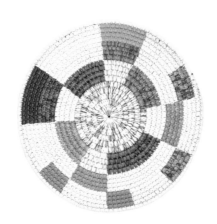

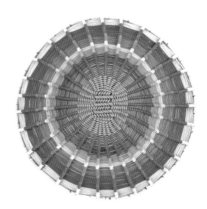
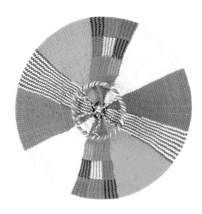

aside on the umsamo (domestic altar) of the home.
Very strict rules and etiquette are followed in the brewing, drinking,
and presentation of the beer. It deserves only the most beautiful containers and lids.
To my mind there is nothing more beautiful than a sumptuous
fat clay ukhamba burnished to a magnificent shine,
in the deepest black of the amadlozi,
elegantly decorated with just a few amasumpa
(a traditional decorative element of raised "warts" or bumps) here and there,
and crowned with a beautifully made grass imbenge, which has been lovingly
decorated by the woman of the house in the colors of the clan.

During the rural depression of the 1970s attempts were made to revitalize
the vanishing basket-making craft in Zululand in order to create jobs.
But plastic containers had long since replaced the various
baskets that were traditionally used around the home.
The only basket still being made was the imbenge.
It was probably the amadlozi then, who had refused to let that tradition die. Entrepreneurs
who went to the countryside and the hostels to sell plastic
beer pots soon declared bankruptcy; and the small enamel bowls they offered
just could not replace the izimbenge as covers for the pots.
These imbenge-making skills survived and it was soon possible to resurrect the craft, and
expand market for these baskets, which today has become the main source of livelihood
for the thousands of brave mothers and grandmothers
who are the backbone of our rural communities.

Not that time stood still for these objects or communities.
Nguni culture is totally inclusive, constantly on the lookout for new skills and
materials, new ways of doing things; of making them even more exciting and beautiful.
This quest applies to dress, to dance, to music, and to crafts.
One can imagine the return of the prodigal son from iGoli—Johannesburg,
Gauteng, the city of gold—where he had toiled underground in the mines for a year.
He would be laden with technological wonders: a radio,
a wind-up gramophone, widely flared, multicolored bell-bottom trousers,
many glass beads, and a roll of telephone wire. This was grass of another sort.
As thin as the finest grass, stronger than the ilala palm leaves, and more
colorful than the best dyes obtained from local roots and leaves
or even those from the chemist (pharmacist) in the nearest town.

opposite page, top row, left to right:
**WOVEN PALM IMBENGE**
Artist unknown
285 mm diameter, Collection of Marisa Fick-Jordaan

**WOVEN PALM IMBENGE WITH BEADS**
Artist unknown
185 x 85 mm, Collection of Marisa Fick-Jordaan

**WOVEN WOOL IMBENGE**
Artist unknown
180 x 70 mm, Collection of the Phansi Museum

middle row, left to right:
**TELEPHONE-WIRE IMBENGE**
Artist unknown
190mm diameter, Private Collection

**IMBENGE WITH TELEPHONE-WIRE OVER GRASS**
Artist unknown
190 mm diameter, Private Collection

**TELEPHONE-WIRE IMBENGE**
Artist unknown
210 mm diameter, Private Collection

bottom row, left to right:
**TELEPHONE-WIRE IMBENGE WITH LOOPED EDGE**
Artist unknown
280 mm diameter, Collection of Marisa Fick-Jordaan

**TELEPHONE-WIRE IMBENGE**
Artist unknown
200 x 80 mm, Collection of Marisa Fick-Jordaan

**TELEPHONE-WIRE IMBENGE**
Artist unknown
175 mm diameter, Collection of the Phansi Museum, Durban

Until the introduction of the core of mild steel wire, small bundles of grass continued to be used as the coil, as they had in the past. The telephone wire, which replaced the ilala *palm*, was used to decorate and bind the basket together.

Traditionally baskets of all sorts were made by men, and only very occasionally by women, and were sold at local markets.
These baskets would then be taken home and decorated with beadwork by the women.
The decorations were individual and the decorator more or less exuberant, but the women would generally use only certain color codes and local symbols of the region and or the clan.
The codes themselves might change over time, with the exclusion or addition of colors, symbols, or writing.
These changes make for a fascinating study and help to identify and locate baskets and beadwork in particular clan areas and in time.

Why the codes change is often difficult to establish.
For instance, we still do not understand why the seven colors of the isishunka pattern used in the Msinga region of KwaZulu-Natal suddenly made way for the isithembu colors, with the addition of bright yellow, and then later for the simpler but more colorful umzansi *patterns*, or the phalafini *pattern*, for that matter.
Each is distinct and different and associated with small local clan villages or the shop or event at which they may have originated.
Other trails are easier to follow.
When, for some reason—war, lack of transport, deteriorating roads, poverty—the people of the highlands stop trading with those in the lowlands, the age-old exchange of grasses and palm leaves stops.
Replacement materials have to be found.
One is wool, which is strong, colorful, and available.
The use of a new material soon results in new designs and new, local color codes. Beads are no longer essential as the decoration may be stitched right into the object.

above, top:
**CLAY BEER POT WITH GRASS *IMBENGE* COVERED WITH BEADS**
175 x 225 mm (pot), 60 x 180 mm (*imbenge*), Collection of Jim Rimelspach

above, bottom:
**COILED TELEPHONE WIRE OVER GRASS BOWL**
Artist unknown
345 x 175 mm, Collection of the Phansi Museum, Durban

None of those changes and inevitable developments altered the traditional function of the imbenge. The real revolution occurred in Johannesburg, that much hated, much loved city, the origin of everything, all the evil in the world and all the knowledge, and the rural communities' link to the universe.
iGoli is where all real men spent their youth and acquired their wisdom, be it political, technological, or artistic. It is where decisions were made about hairstyles and about how much knee a young married woman should show under her cowhide

marriage skirt. From here great global ideas, gathered from movies,
abafundisi (teachers), friends, and magazines, were transformed
and transferred to the remotest corners of the rural areas.

Working with metal had always been the domain and the responsibility of men
as has been the caring for the cattle, erecting the structure of the home,
working with grass and leather, and providing the security of the family at home.
It was traditionally women who worked with earth, made the pots, plastered the huts,
planted the crops, did the beadwork, brewed the beer, cooked, and had the children. The
new metal imbenge fitted well into this division of labor.
Most of South Africa's gold mines are clustered around the Witwatersrand, with
Johannesburg as the fulcrum. Each mine was operated as a fiefdom,
with a mine manager in charge of a small town totally dedicated to it.
Management and skilled staff lived in colonial luxury.
The hard underground work was mostly reserved for migrant laborers from the rural areas,
who worked on short-term contracts and lived in single-sex hostels.
This system, first begun on the diamond mines in Kimberly during the 1870s,
continues to this day, although in a more humane and dignified way.
While it produced many social ills, it did produce a society in
which the allocation of jobs by gender could not exist.
There were no women to make pots, do the beadwork, cook, or sew.
Soon the most wonderfully decorated patchwork clothes
and decorated baskets were being produced.

The domain of the male was perpetuated when the baskets were decorated
with the colorful wire and sewing machines were used to make the clothes.
Cooking became the grilling of meat and steaming of maize meal—South Africa's favorite
meal to this day—eaten standing up. Honor could thus be maintained.
Only pottery remained in the female domain and soon a thriving trade developed,
with the clay izinkhamba (beer pots) being delivered to the miners, and the decorated
wire izimbenge being made in iGoli and exported back to the villages.
In this way the humble imbenge now found its way back home totally transformed, much
more beautiful and durable; and it was no longer
necessary to have the women decorate it to make it special.
Many other materials were tried along the way, among them plastic bags
cut into strips, sisal string, and garden nursery twine, but these did not find a market. Only
the scoobie wire and the grass izimbenge survive today.

above, top:
**HORN, WOOD, COPPER WIRE & TELEPHONE WIRE SNUFF BOTTLES**
Artist unknown, h: 150 mm and 130 mm, Private Collection

above, bottom:
**TELEPHONE-WIRE HARD HAT**
Shadercke Ntuli
280 x 220 x 130 mm, Private Collection

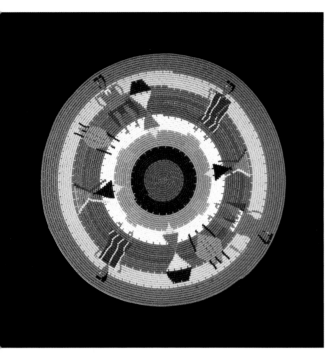

**TELEPHONE-WIRE PLATE**
Bheki Dlamini
310 mm diameter
Collection of David Arment

Originally the mines were organized and organized themselves by tribe and clan,
and the old traditions were adhered to, each home area retaining
its own color and design combinations and preferences.
In izimbenge *from the Umvoti area, for instance, white and blue wire was used.*
*Closer to Durban, very strong geometric designs were preferred.*
*The items were sold at special markets, of which the Mai Mai market*
*in central Johannesburg was probably the most famous.*
*It was at this market that the prodigal son would stock up before returning home.*
*A large* kist, *beautifully decorated, with mirrors and glued-on prints of the*
*Kaiser Chiefs soccer team or of Jesus and Mary, or both, would be loaded with*
*beads, blankets,* izimbenge, *and other wonders of technology made from the finest materi-*
*als available—plastic and Perspex—insulation tape in different colors, bicycle reflectors,*
*maybe even a bicycle, aluminum wire, and many other treasures.*
*It was expected of a young man, especially if he were returning to get married,*
*to be generous to his own and his future wife's family.*

Wire imbenge *making is hard work, man's work.*
*It takes skill, strength, and time.*
*It was ideal for those who protect and guard us during the long and*
*lonely nights, the night watchmen. Fearless, feared Zulu night watchmen!*
*These were the great, great, great grandchildren of the majestic Cetshwayo,*
*who whipped the British army at iSandlwana in 1879.*
*Wire weaving became their industry.*
*While some specialized in the covering of bottles and knobkerries*
*(sticks used as weapons), most went for the* imbenge *market.*
*They shared their skills willingly and one would often see small groups of*
*heavily clad night watchmen in their cast-off army greatcoats clustered*
*around a fire made in a cut-off, perforated oil drum, keeping warm and working*
*at their beautiful baskets, discussing designs and techniques and, one hoped, keeping an*
*ear out and eyes open for the odd* scebenga (bad guy), *who would be trying to get into the*
*back door, possibly to steal telephone wire to sell to night watchmen.*

One can picture similar groups of men, centuries ago, even before
Shaka founded the nation, in deepest Zululand, also sitting around the fire,
keeping warm and decorating their dancing and
walking sticks with copper, bronze, and iron wire.
Melting, casting, and hammering the metal, they were producing

brass beads, gauntlets, arm rings, wire, and spears.
They were always on the lookout for new metals and other material for decorations.
Iron was mined locally, but most other treasures trickled in from north and east
Africa or from the missionaries and later from the colonial merchants in barter trade. Many
an elephant was sacrificed on the altar of vanity.

When I and many others discovered the izimbenge, we were taken
by their beauty and entirely dismissed their function.
We preferred the inside of the imbenge—turned over, it is like a bowl—and
tended to look at the designs from that side.
We wanted them to hang on the wall—they were just too beautiful to be hidden away—and
we wanted them bigger and flatter; the baskets were becoming plates.
At night we waited outside Fast Sails, a small factory, to find out if
Elliot Mkhize or Bheki Dlamini had produced another masterpiece.
Or we would go to the African Art Centre in Durban to find out if
another genius basket maker had been discovered.
For more than two decades, the proprietors of the Art Centre had nurtured the
grass-roots artists and encouraged them to show and sell their work to a wider public.
Most of the artists were very poor, often out of work, and struggled to buy the wire. When
times were particularly bad, in the 1980s, I even "inherited" a number
of homeless basket makers, who settled in at my architecture offices.
Then in 1992 we launched the Bartel Arts Trust (BAT), funding an art center
and development projects, workshops, and residential facilities.
Soon a whole group of wire-basket makers moved there
and we could reclaim our office.

Some brought their wives and children and
soon the gender barrier was entirely dissolved.
Women were making wire baskets and two young men,
Thami Jali and Clive Sithole, were making wonderful pots!
Marisa Fick-Jordaan established the BAT Shop and took over.
She wanted the baskets bigger still, and flatter, and wilder.
She pushed the artists and found the buyers.
She gave them all courage and helped them unearth their talents—
and soon they took flight and magic happened and a new art form was born.

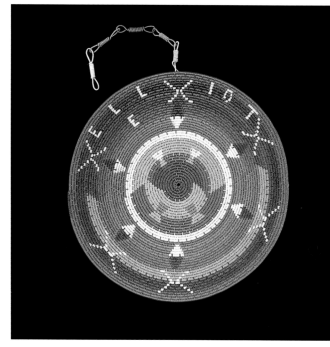

**"ELLIOT" BASKET**
Elliot Mkhize
210 mm diameter
Collection of the Phansi Museum, Durban

# TRANSITIONS

1

by Marisa Fick-Jordaan

When Bartel Arts Trust (BAT) and Nedbank Arts and Culture Trust were launched simultaneously in 1994, this was the major arts event of the year in South Africa. And when Paul Mikula, the founding trustee of the Bartel Arts Trust, appeared in full Batman regalia on the stage, the arts community was delighted. This momentous happening was certainly eclipsed by the inauguration of Nelson Mandela as the first democratically elected president of post-apartheid South Africa, and this election brought a newfound sense of optimism to the country after decades of despair and isolation.

A few months later, I went to the BAT Centre to buy my first telephone-wire basket. Ducking under scaffolding and climbing over piles of concrete bricks, I managed to locate Bheki Dlamini and his pregnant wife, Dudu Cele, in a back room adjacent to the future visual arts studio. Then, with Dudu's *Hello South Africa* basket under my arm, I bumped into Mike van Graan, the director of BAT, who jokingly asked if I were looking for a job. "Never!" I replied. Not eight months later I would be persuaded to set up the BAT Shop and telephone-wire weaving would become part of my daily existence and an all-consuming passion. Never is a long time, as they say.

opposite page:
**HELLO SOUTH AFRICA**
Dudu Cele
285 mm diameter
Collection of Marisa Fick-Jordaan

**THE BAT CENTRE**
Small Craft Harbor, Durban
Photograph by Angie Buckland

My foray into the craft world started when, as a fashion designer in the early 1990s, I had started exploring the possibility of using Zulu beadwork for clothing that was to be marketed under the African Legacy label. There were hardly any books available for reference, so for inspiration I borrowed old beadwork pieces from Jo Thorpe, the doyenne of African art, who was then at the African Art Centre. Expecting Jo to disapprove of my commercial, trendy interpretations of a cultural legacy, I was surprised when she encouraged me, saying that the Zulu crafters were ready to work in new directions.

In the first week after the shop opened, Bheki Dlamini arrived with a handful of students from the Siyanda community—Albert Dlamini, Anamaria Dlamini, Zodwa Maphumulo, Ntombifuthi Magwasa, and Elliot Ndwandwe—all urging me to buy their wire baskets. The master weaver Elliot Mkhize soon brought his wares and many early photographs show this little band proudly posing in front of the cobalt blue wall that was dedicated to showcasing what, to my mind, was the most distinctive, vibrant, exciting, contemporary art form.

All the early baskets were of the traditional *imbenge* (beer pot) size, very small, around 190 millimeters in diameter, and although here and there a figure, a car, or a hut appeared, the predominant motif was variations of what we called the Zulu *imbali* (flower), a pattern of radiating rings with points or petals. To make their work more marketable, we showed the weavers books, including carpet designs and art and design magazines to inspire them to work in new shapes and sizes. With some direction on design, the weavers began developing more complex geometric patterns that were initially inspired by Zulu beadwork, particularly the complex patterns from the Nongoma district and Zulu earplug designs from Msinga.

The annual BAT calendars celebrating traditional Zulu artifacts became a major source of inspiration and were proudly displayed in urban shacks and rural homesteads. Exhibitions at the BAT Centre showcasing the best examples of traditional Zulu material culture from private collections encouraged a renewed pride in local design. When additional colors became available, as a result of the BAT Shop ordering custom hues from suppliers, traditional combinations were used, but later weavers began to experiment with a wider color palette as these were also made available. We placed an emphasis on the development of individuality, and the weavers began producing increasingly sophisticated and intricate abstract geometric designs, working well outside the boundaries of traditional Zulu patterning.

Each name was prominently displayed when baskets were placed for sale or on exhibit at the BAT Shop. By giving credit to the weavers, we were encouraging them to develop an individual style and attribution became a useful tool when we were obliged to decline work of poor quality. Often we were offered baskets that had been woven in unattractive and dull colors, but they included innovative design elements and we began to understand that the basic materials of this craft were difficult to obtain. Scrap-metal merchants were hounded for "scoobie wire," the PVC-coated copper telephone wire that the weavers were using. In my naiveté, celebrating the innovative use of a recycled material, I had no idea at the time of the side effects of this craft: the increasing theft of copper-wire cables and the problems the theft caused in the entire community, but more immediately to Telkom, the company that provided telephone service in the country, and to the rural farmers who depended on it. International patrons appreciated and purchased the baskets; the locals, including government officials, had to be appeased for the resulting disruption in telephone service.

In May 1996 I was asked to curate WIRED, the first exhibition of telephone-wire baskets in the Menzi Gallery at the BAT Centre. The media publicity and critical acclaim for the exhibition helped to create a wider local audience. As sales increased rapidly, so did our group of Siyanda weavers. Twenty minutes drive from Durban, Siyanda (the optimistic name means "we are moving forward") is a sprawling informal settlement adjacent to one of the largest townships outside the city of Durban. The core residents of the community settled in Siyanda after political violence during the 1980s forced them to abandon their original homes. Supported by the BAT Shop, this community has become the center of telephone-wire weaving. Within two years, the weaving group had grown to about seventy people and several imaginative and talented artists emerged from this community.

The craft spread when neighbors and family members were taught to weave, and despite the attitude of most newly urbanized young men toward what they perceived to be "women's work," they, too, appreciated the possibility of staying at home, using their hands, and earning incomes—a far cry from waiting to pick up employment here and there in the formal sector. Unlike other craft forms that are practiced exclusively by either men or women, and in which skills are passed down through tradition, the Siyanda project was, and remains, the domain of a disparate group of men and women of all ages, most of whom had no prior crafting skills.

Acknowledging the growing market for distinctly South African products, and realizing the potential for generating an income by producing handmade craftwork, the South African government decided to make the so-called cultural industries a priority. The government began providing financial support for training and encouraging partnerships with internal and external development agencies. From the start, the modernization of the craft and the

**THE INFORMAL SETTLEMENT OF SIYANDA**
Outside of Durban, South Africa
Photograph by David Arment

development of the products were driven by the market. Feedback from the market was crucial: product, price, quality, and on-time delivery are what the market wants. The BAT Shop has helped to build the market by encouraging the weavers to be innovative, to expand their designs, and to produce baskets of high quality. We also believe that it is important to build sustainable relationships with all the people we deal with.

As a result of the initial success, the group had grown too big to go on as it had begun, with a mentor for each weaver. To continue improving the designs and quality of the baskets, we asked the Masibambane Trust, which was established to support economic development projects, to fund formal workshops at the BAT Centre. Elliot Mkhize was brought in to teach technique, and we made suggestions about the design of the baskets and offered lessons on the important issue of money management. In 1998 our efforts were rewarded when Ntombifuthi Magwasa won the prestigious FNB Vita Craft Now Award for her wire basket. Telephone-wire basketry had made the leap from curio to art craft.

For our first attempts at what might be called mass production, the weavers were asked to repeat designs that had proved popular in the shop. Once the weavers could reproduce those designs to a standard size, we presented a sample of their work to the interior designer Boyd Ferguson, of the interior design firm Cecile and Boyd, who was at the time designing the innovative Singita Lodge, located in the Sabi Sand Reserve, adjacent to the Kruger National Park in South Africa. What we showed him was a flat tray with a rim. His response was entirely enthusiastic and has led to one of our most successful and continuing collaborations. The tray itself, which is used as a decorative under plate for the table settings, has become a classic product that has been mentioned in many editorials on the subject of design and illustrated in articles about the interior design of the lodge. As Cecile and Boyd have worked on new lodges for the Singita Private Game Reserve, new designs have been developed for the under plates and, because they are offered for sale in the boutiques attached to the lodges, they are providing a steady income for the weavers while gracing tables around the world.

In 1997 the French contemporary artist Hervé Di Rosa traveled to South Africa at the invitation of the newly established French Institute of South Africa. After visits to Johannesburg and Cape Town, he arrived at the BAT Centre in search of master crafters with whom he could collaborate on his project *Autour du Monde*. Finding that Johannesburg and Cape Town were relatively devoid of traditional craft, he was enthusiastic about the number of people practicing Zulu crafts in the Durban area. Here he saw people working in several traditional and transitional techniques, from wood burning and

opposite:

**THE ELEMENTS OF LIFE**, 1998

Design by Hervé Di Rosa

Woven by Zodwa Maphumulo

800 mm diameter, Private Collection

Photograph by Pierre Schwatrz

sculpting to plastic-bag weaving. Initially he wanted to use them all, but in the end he focused on telephone-wire weaving, beadwork, and wood carving. He launched a collaboration titled Dirozulu. In selecting Durban and BAT as the eighth step of his world tour, he was also drawn by the diverse Asian, Zulu, and European influences on the cultural landscape of Durban—its harbor reminded him, he said, of Sète, the city in the south of France where he had been born.

Although the baskets in their contemporary form are artworks, the weavers had not ventured much beyond the original bowl or lid shape. Hervé needed a larger, more traditionally flat canvas for his designs and had no interest in the functional applications of the technique. He was able to expand the possibilities of the form and to increase the diameter of the new, mandala shape from about thirty to ninety centimeters (approximately twelve to thirty-five inches), but his innovation was limited by the circular weaving process, which prescribed the shape of his canvas and elements of his designs. He also discovered that telephone-wire weaving technique is quite rigid in its possibilities and that certain forms and intervals that were an intrinsic part of his designs were simply impossible to make. So he adapted the designs and, when all the bumps were ironed out, the process picked up momentum. Small mock-ups of the new designs were made and then enlarged at a printing shop. Hervé then specified the design parameters, selected a telephone-wire palette of around fifteen colors, and art happened, a cross-fertilization of universal imagery and local icons. The fruits of Di Rosa's two-year collaboration with Vincent Sithole, Simon Mavundla, Alice Gcaba, Zodwa Maphumulo, and Elliot Ndwandwe, were exhibited in May 2000 at the Menzi Gallery at the BAT Centre and in July 2000 at the Standard Bank Gallery in Johannesburg. Shortly thereafter two Dirozulu mandalas were included in *Passage d'exotisme,* the fifth Lyon Biennale. I served as project director for the collaboration, an experience that expanded my view of the possibilities for the baskets in terms of both scale and design.

On a visit to Mdukutshani in rural Msinga, I discovered not only a kindred spirit in Creina Alcock, who was leading a similar design and marketing project, but also the existence of a telephone-wire weaving project at Waayhoek, near Ladysmith in central KwaZulu-Natal, midway between Durban and Johannesburg. In 1988 Tessa Katzenellembogen had taught flood survivors from the Waayhoek resettlement community to weave telephone-wire bowls using the soft-wire technique traditionally used by Zulu night watchmen to cover sticks and to make *izimbenge* (beer-pot lids). This soft-wire technique, by which the wire is woven around a mold or template, is less labor intensive than the coiled technique used

opposite page, clockwise from top left:
**BLACK-AND-WHITE SOFT-WIRE "AZTEC" BOWL**
Themba Ndlovu
110 x 305 mm
Collection of Magda van der Vloed

**"BAT SHOP MARISA FICK"**
Subusiso Dholodo
310 mm diameter
Collection of Marisa Fick-Jordaan

**LAMPSHADE BOWL**
zenzulu
380 mm diameter
Private Collection

**BLACK-AND-WHITE PLATE**
Doris Mkhize
285 mm diameter
Collection of Marisa Fick-Jordaan

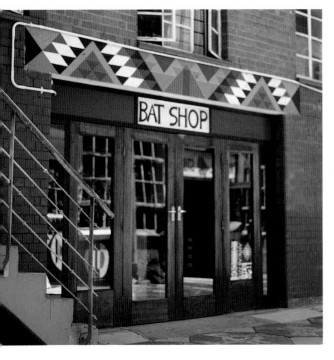

**THE BAT SHOP**
Durban, South Africa

for both the under plates mentioned above and the coiled, hard-wire, master-weave baskets. Many of the traditional zigzag-design bowls produced by the Waayhoek community were marketed to galleries in Johannesburg and to international museum stores.

By the time I found out about this group, Tessa was living in London, and many of the weavers had, as a result of violence and problems with land settlement in the area, moved back to Msinga, where they had lived before being forcibly moved under apartheid. In addition to the zigzag-design bowls, Tessa had developed eggs and bowls made of copper wire and glass beads, and under Creina's watchful eye and direction, these objects have become classics in South African and international craft markets. Hoping to find a new market for this work, we arranged that the BAT Shop would sell a set of four small bowls in various styles and colors, some of solid colors, some with a simple swirl design in two or more colors. This was our first step in the design of a commercial range of baskets.

In 1998 representatives from Black Dog, a newly formed company based in Paris marketing craft products from South Africa, visited Durban. Recognizing the potential to expand the range offered by the BAT Shop, they offered to help develop a very different object: a large bowl with a flat bottom, a shape we have named our lampshade design, which would fuse traditional craft skills with minimalist contemporary design.

At the time, only two weavers were skilled in this technique of weaving the telephone wire over a mold, there was only one master mold, and the supply of materials was limited. The design concepts proved a challenge even to the masterful Jaheni Mkhize. Nonetheless, a mold manufacturer was found and funding made available for the development of skills. Contracted to run a series of workshops to teach new weavers, Jaheni managed to expand the project to include twenty members of the Mkhize family and several friends from the Greytown area, about three hours from Durban.

These lampshade baskets were initially marketed only through Black Dog, and were bought by Donna Karan for her store in New York and were sold at the Musée des arts décoratifs in Paris. After two years, with production capacity at a minimum and demand growing, the BAT Shop took control of marketing, registered the name zenzulu as a trademark, and continues to update and expand the range annually. The objects produced by this design symbiosis have received many accolades, including an Elle Decoration International Design Award in 2002. For recent designs, glass beads and natural seeds have been used together with the telephone wire, and the colors are continuously updated. The design has also been used in a range of fashion accessories and Christmas ornaments.

In late 1998 a visit by the Australian curator Christina McGuiness to establish an artist's exchange program with the Artists Foundation of Western Australia, led to an invitation to attend and exhibit at the Perth International Arts Festival in 2000. Only two artists would be attending and, in an attempt to keep the selection democratic, we arranged a competition and exhibition to coincide with our annual BAT Shop end-of-year party. The Masibambane Trust stepped forward with a generous offer for the prize money. After much deliberation by an independent jury, the work of Vincent Sithole and Ntombifuthi Magwasa was selected and they were invited to Perth. The competition proved to be a great motivation to many other emerging weavers. Zama Khanyile, for instance, won a merit award for a small basket that was to give a taste of what was to come later in her career.

The start of the new millennium saw us winging our way to Australia with enough wire baskets, as well as a few recycled-tin cars and airplanes, to fill the two gallery floors of the Moore's Building in Fremantle. After two years of planning and fundraising, the *Durbs to Freo Wire and Metal Act* became a reality. Arriving on Australia Day, the two Zulu artists had their first taste of a full-blown fireworks display. We were all feted and in the media spotlight for two weeks. With bumper attendances and a sellout show, our first international exhibition was a resounding success.

Invited by the French Institute to curate an exhibition, *Contemporary Zulu Basketry,* at the Alliance Française Gallery in Johannesburg at the end of 2000, we managed to extend the scope of the exhibition to include traditional *ilala* palm basketry from Hlabisa and copper-wire baskets from Msinga. Since its inception, the BAT Shop had forged close ties with the well-known *ilala* palm basket weavers in northern KwaZulu-Natal. The Masibambane Trust again provided the prize money to be awarded for the best baskets at the exhibition. The emerging master weaver Simon Mavundla took the honors in the telephone-wire section. Elias Mtshengu and Ngakhelaphi Mkhize, members of the original Waayhoek project, won the first and second prizes for their copper-wire baskets.

A fortuitous visit to the *Contemporary Zulu Basketry* exhibition by the director of the OXO Tower Wharf and Gallery, in London, served as inspiration for the suggestion that an exhibition of contemporary South African craft might form part of the promotional Celebrate South Africa month in London and throughout the United Kingdom. Works by Alice Gcaba and an installation of the BAT Shop's zenzulu range of contemporary wire baskets were selected for the exhibition, titled *Bowled Over,* that opened at the OXO Gallery in May 2001.

"BAT CENTA"
Tholiwe Ntsele
370 mm diameter
Collection of Marisa Fick-Jordaan

Spreading our wings even further that year, we were invited, sponsored under the Chicago Sister Cities International Program, to exhibit and be the cultural anchor at "Listen to Africa," a conference aimed at highlighting sustainable and innovative development in Africa. This became a memorable experience in more ways than one, as we arrived in Chicago the night before the planes slammed into the Twin Towers on the morning of September 11, 2001. We would like to believe that the colorful telephone-wire baskets on show helped to lift spirits in the aftermath of the tragic events that affected us all.

Continuing the tradition of excellence, Zama Khanyile and Vincent Sithole have joined Ntombifuthi Magwasa and Elliot Mkhize on the FNB Vita Craft Now Awards roll of honor. More opportunities to exhibit internationally are opening up as collectors and museums increasingly acknowledge that the boundaries between what is called *art* and what is called *craft* are being blurred, given that the latter is as valid as the former in representing authentic and vital expression.

Notwithstanding its direction and expansion of the design of objects, the BAT Shop continues to acknowledge and, more importantly, to nurture the unique and original creativity of the artists it works with. Despite harsh social conditions, many creative individuals have managed to put their talents to productive use. Crafters are earning sustainable incomes and many of them are the sole breadwinners in extended families. After decades of benign neglect, Siyanda is being transformed under an urban-renewal program. Water and electricity are being installed, the roads improved, and brick-and-mortar houses will replace the shack dwellings. This is exciting and long overdue, of course, but in some way it is sad in that much of the textured character, individual expression, and innovation in the use of building materials will necessarily disappear. Weaving skills are now being passed on to the next generation. In ten years, coiled telephone-wire basket weaving has become a traditional craft in an urban area where none existed before. My hope is that chickens will continue to scratch in the dust and that the design inspiration that has long been drawn from rural pasts will not be lost as Siyanda itself changes.

opposite:
**COLORFUL SWIRL & ZIGZAG BOWLS**
zenzulu
Private Collection

# THE MASTER WEAVERS 2

What began as a craft of utility has become, through the dedication of a small group of weavers in a rural community in Zululand, an art form. With the encouragement of their advocates and collectors, a few weavers have taken this craft to the next level, creating a uniquely African artistic expression.

Many people now weave baskets, but a few talented artists have risen above the rest, weaving wire into art. We call them the master weavers, the artists who have contributed something very special to this form. It is they who are appreciated as today's finest weavers of telephone wire.

It started with a few weavers who really were the night watchmen, Elliot Mkhize, Bheki Dlamini, and Alfred Ntuli. Later, masters such as Zodwa Maphumulo, Dudu Cele, Ntombifuthi Magwasa, Alice Gcaba, and Robert Majola joined the ranks and quickly received recognition in South Africa and internationally. Now those pioneers have been joined by a new group of weavers whose work has a contemporary flair: Simon Mavundla, Vincent Sithole, Zama Khanyile, Bheki Sibiya, Jaheni Mkhize, and Mboniseni Khanyile.

opposite page:
**JAHENI MKHIZE DEMONSTRATING THE SOFT-WIRE WEAVING TECHNIQUE**
Photographed at the BAT Centre, January 2004

Not only do these master weavers provide a legacy of beautiful baskets, but also they have been instrumental in handing down their skills to their friends, family, and the next generation. This is truly an African form of community development, the key to the craft economy that provides income and self-sufficiency for a large community of weavers. These are the masters today, but the art form continues to develop and we look forward to new weavers, who will continue to push the art form forward.

opposite page:
**BHEKI SIBIYA DEMONSTRATING THE
HARD-WIRE WEAVING TECHNIQUE**
Photographed at the BAT Centre,
January 2004

# DUDU CELE

Born 1970, Port Shepstone, KwaZulu-Natal
Died 2002, Durban

Dudu began weaving in the early 1990s, learning to weave from her husband, Bheki Dlamini. Although her initial work was similar to his, it did not take long for her to develop her own patterns and figures, including the integration of more animals and natural themes.

Dudu's work is well described as being full of riotous colors and oozing individual expression. She had a passion for celebrating life and occasion in her work, and her baskets showcase images of soccer championships and other such events. Her soft spot for a little romance shows in the red hearts that creep into many of her designs. One basket pays tribute to Nelson Mandela and Graca Machel, and features a luxury car, a honeymoon hotel, cheerleaders, and the *QE2*, on which the distinguished couple sailed to Cape Town.

Like Bheki, she loved including script in her weaving. Celebratory greetings containing birthday, Valentine, and Christmas wishes were her favorite. Because the quality of her lettering was high and her English literacy skills were good, she was always the first weaver who came to mind when the BAT Shop received private or corporate requests that included lettering.

Dudu is represented in the Durban Art Gallery and Gertrude Posel collections, and in numerous private collections in South Africa and abroad. In 1996 she participated in the group exhibition *Jabulisa: The Art of KwaZulu-Natal,* at the Standard Bank National Arts Festival in Grahamstown. The exhibition also toured to the Durban Art Gallery and the Tatham Art Gallery in Pietermaritzburg. Dudu died of AIDS-related complications in 2002.

Photograph by William Raats

opposite page:
**PLATE COMMEMORATING THE WEDDING
OF NELSON MANDELA & GRACA MACHEL**
Dudu Cele
400 mm diameter, Collection of Marisa Fick-Jordaan

following pages, left, clockwise from top left:
**JUMPING IMPALA**
Dudu Celi
336 mm diameter, Private Collection

**GIRAFFE AND OTHER ANIMALS**
Dudu Celi
300 mm diameter, Collection of Trisha Wilson

**HAPPY BIRTHDAY**
Dudu Celi
390 mm diameter, Collection of Jim Rimelspach

**AMATUWASA**
Dudu Cele
310 mm diameter, Collection of Marisa Fick-Jordaan

following pages, right:
**MAPANSULA DANCE**
Dudu Cele
290 x 275 mm, Collection of Marisa Fick-Jordaan

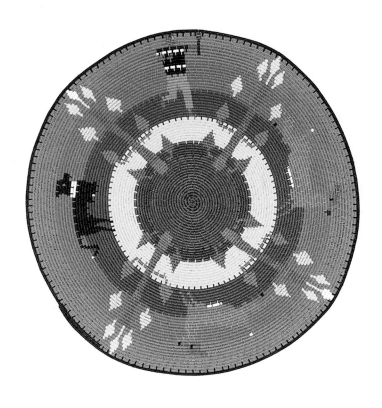
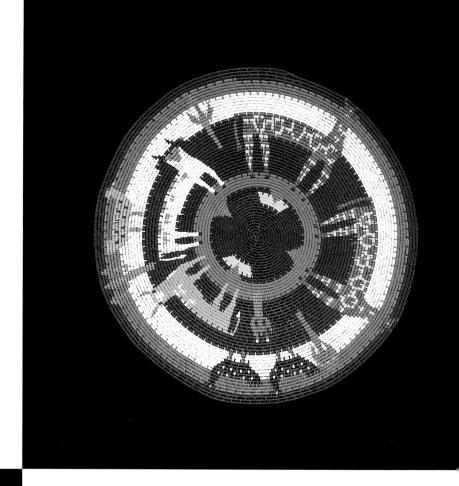
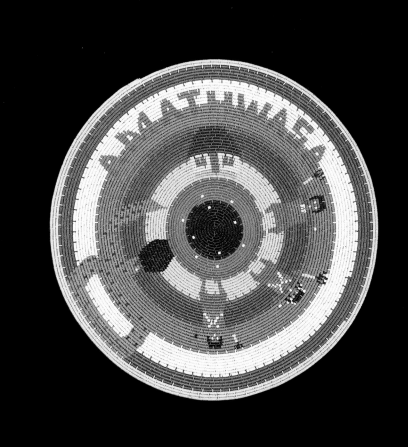

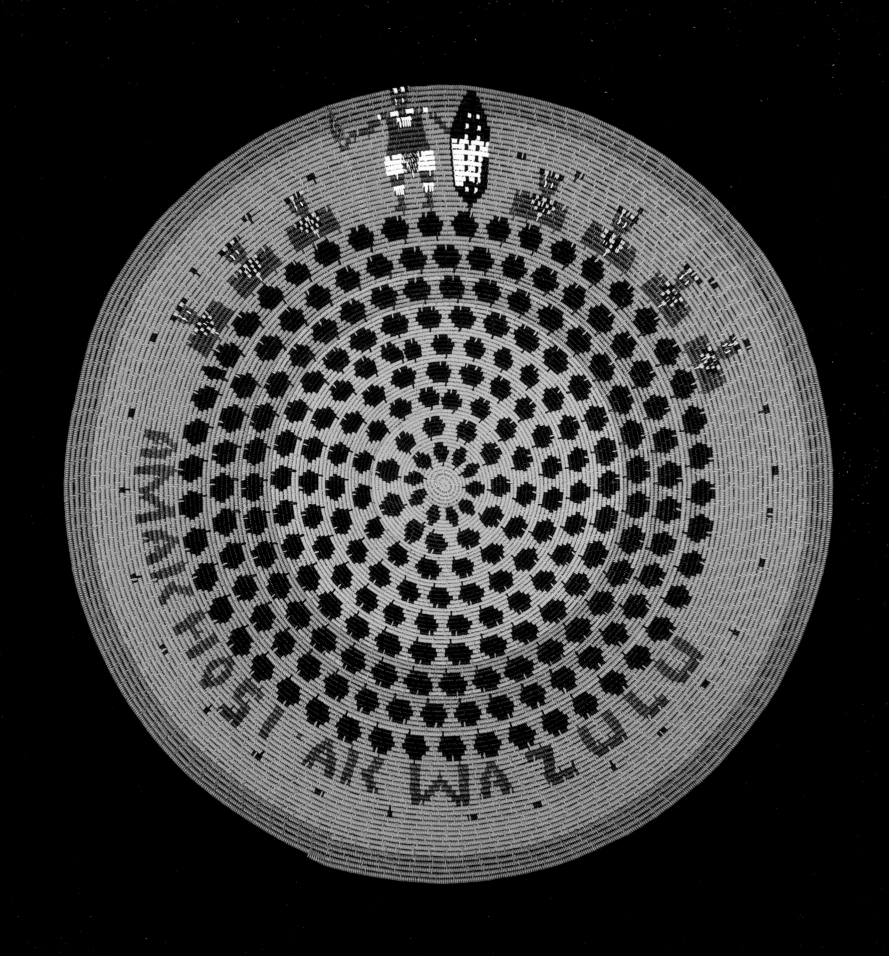

# BHEKI DLAMINI

Born 1957, Esikhawini, KwaZulu-Natal
Died 2003, Durban

Photograph by William Raats

Bheki was a great storyteller who would share his stories for hours with anyone who would listen. Luckily this wonderful ability extended beyond the oral tradition and into his weaving. He began weaving in1987 and was the second master weaver to emerge. When he began weaving he used traditional Zulu patterning, but soon incorporated figurative work and circular rings. Being the first weaver to introduce figures into his designs, he made a name for himself by using the basket as a canvas. Transcending the merely decorative, he wove landscapes and stories into his work, dealing with subjects that ranged from traditional Zulu culture through national sports celebrations.

He was a proud traditionalist, committed to the new South Africa, and a fierce sports fanatic, with a particular love for soccer and big sporting events. His works *Umthakathi, Amathwasa, Bafana Bafana,* and *Rugby World Cup*, among others, spell this out quite loudly. With such zest for life, Bheki was consistently inventing imagery and he never repeated designs. Each of his works is unique.

Also distinctive in Bheki's work was his use of text. He was the first weaver to incorporate it into his works as a matter of course, using the technique to title his designs and as part of the overall storytelling process. While many other weavers found that incorporating script into the design of their baskets was a major challenge, Bheki took up the challenge and made it his trademark.

Bheki's work began to get gallery attention in 1994. That year Kim Saks showed some of his works at an exhibition in her Johannesburg gallery. In 1995 Bheki and his wife, Dudu Cele, were caretakers at the BAT Centre. At the Centre's opening exhibit, Bheki, who came to the opening in traditional Zulu costume, exhibited a bowl that he had woven incorporating a Zulu flower and three figures. He was naturally charming and his talent was so apparent that he quickly became one of the artists most frequently represented in exhibitions. In 1996 he exhibited at the KwaZulu-Natal Biennale, and that same year his work was selected for the South African contemporary art exhibition at the Mermaid Gallery in London. This was his first major recognition.

opposite page:
**AMAKHOSI AKWAZULU**
Bheki Dlamini
470 mm diameter
Collection of David Arment

45

Like many of the weavers, Bheki arrived in Durban to look for a job. Luckily for the residents of Siyanda, he settled there and came to play a pivotal role in their lives. He found work as a delivery man at Fast Sails, a sail-manufacturing business in Durban. There, during his breaks, he socialized with Elliot Mkhize, a security guard who made use of the time by weaving. Bheki watched, learning the skills. Back in Siyanda he shared these skills with others, and became pivotal to the early growth of the craft.

Bheki died of cancer in 2003. He lives on in his work, in his storytelling, and in the new traditions of the wire-weaving skills he shared with many of his fellow weavers.

opposite page, clockwise from top left:
**UMSHADO WESIZULU**
Bheki Dlamini
500 mm diameter
Collection of the Phansi Museum, Durban

**ZULU WARRIORS**
Bheki Dlamini
412 mm diameter
Private Collection

**PARTY TIME**
Bheki Dlamini
342 mm diameter
Collection of Trisha Wilson

**UDWENDWE LUKAKOTO**
Bheki Dlamini
368 mm diameter
Private Collection

following pages, left:
**MADIBA (NELSON MANDELA) AND GRACA GO TO PARLIAMENT**
Bheki Dlamini
470 mm diameter
Collection of Marisa Fick-Jordaan

following pages, right:
**BOWL WTH ZULU FLOWER PATTERN AND FIGURES**
Bheki Dlamini
130 x 130 mm
Collection of Marisa Fick-Jordaan

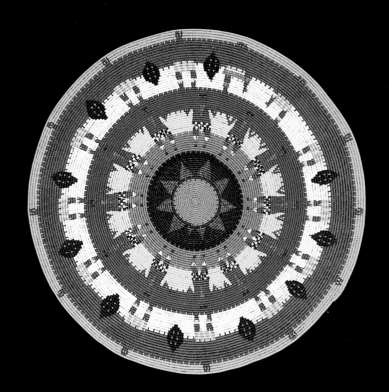

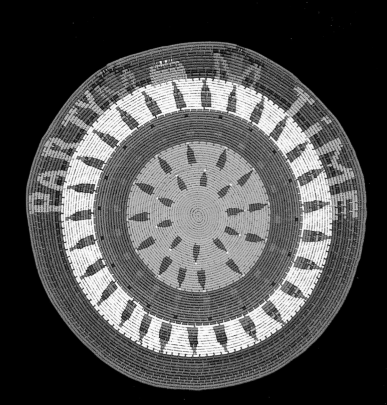

# ALICE GCABA

Born 1956, Flagstaff, Eastern Cape

Alice grew up in a rural community, left school after grade four, and began helping her family with the farming. In1975 she moved from the Eastern Cape to Durban, looking for employment. She found domestic work in Greenwood Park, where she worked for twenty years until her employers died. After their deaths she survived by working as a hawker in Durban, until she began producing telephone-wire baskets in 1996.

In Durban, Alice moved from the rural community of Inanda to KwaMashu (a suburb outside Durban), before settling in Siyanda, where she was one of the first residents. Luckily, she settled next door to Mavis Njokweni, who, like so many of the other weavers in Siyanda, generously shared her skills with Alice. A year later, Alice began selling her work to the BAT Shop.

Her style of baskets is unmistakable. Typically she uses a bright base color and adds many randomly placed figures to her plates and bowls. She weaves the icons of her South African world, both rural and urban, into her baskets, and her figures include people, huts, houses, lizards, and various other animals. When she works with patterns she often uses an interesting interplay of colors between positive and negative. Consistently working with bright and vibrant colors, Alice has created a quirky style.

In addition to her figurative design elements, Alice has become a master of form, creating not only plates, but also a deep and precise hard-wire bowl. This shape is a challenge to weave, and Alice does it with ease.

An independent woman who lives alone, Alice provides for herself and also supports her extended family back in the Eastern Cape. Like many of the other weavers, she has taught a core of Siyanda women to weave.

opposite page:
**LARGE BLACK PLATE WITH FIGURES**
Alice Gcaba
476 mm diameter, Collection of David Arment

following pages, left:
**RED PLATE WITH FIGURES**
Alice Gcaba
362 mm diameter, Private Collection

**WHITE PLATE WITH FIGURES**
Alice Gcaba
420 mm diameter, Collection of David Arment

**PURPLE BOWL WITH FIGURES**
Alice Gcaba
368 mm diameter, Collection of David Arment

**BLUE PLATE WITH FIGURES**
Alice Gcaba
420 mm diameter, Private Collection

following pages, right:
**PURPLE BOWL WITH FIGURES**
Alice Gcaba
368 mm diameter, Collection of David Arment

# ZAMA KHANYILE

Born 1971, Empangeni

Zama's story is one of perseverance, and is the stuff of fairy tales—a politically correct Cinderella-meets-Pygmalion story. Zama had a low-wage job at a restaurant at Durban Station. She wished for better things and always kept an eye open for something better. And one day it came to her. She read a news story about Ntombifuthi Magwasa, a settlement dweller who had won the big FNB Vita Craft Now Award for her telephone-wire baskets.

Zama immediately began weaving baskets to try to sell to the BAT Shop. Her early baskets were, in a word, *terrible*, and the BAT Shop bought none. For six months she persisted, making poor-quality baskets and begging the buyers to take her wares, "even for little money." She would arrive on sale days, timid, her face all but obscured under a hat, lurk behind all the other weavers, and hide her mouth behind her hand when she spoke. But she never gave up.

Then came the competition to select entries for the Perth International Arts Festival. The judges spotted a basket they liked. It displayed quality and a good sense of design. In a word, it was beautiful. So it was selected, and off it went to Perth. When Marisa checked the pricing on the basket, she found that Zama, so used to disappointment, had severely underpriced it. Marisa raised the price by 400 percent and it sold. In addition, Zama won a small cash prize in the competition.

After the festival, Zama arrived to be paid for her basket. When she received her money, she burst into tears. It was the most money she had ever earned in her life, and probably one of the first times she had ever felt validated. She has been weaving incredible baskets ever since. She began experimenting with imagery and soon after made a basket decorated with cows. After that, Marisa showed her some wrapping paper illustrated with leopards. She incorporated the animals into her next work, complete with three-dimensional whiskers. Subsequently she produced a series of spotted-cat baskets, and now,

opposite page:

**PLATE WITH MULTICOLOR CATS**
Zama Khanyile
508 mm diameter
Collection of David Arment

working on quite a large scale, includes figures, birds, and trees. It seems there is no stopping Zama, whose name, incidentally, means "to try"!

Since her success in Perth and receiving a merit award at the FNB Vita Craft Now Awards in 2002, Zama's work has become much sought after and she has become a full-time weaver. Her confidence level has increased along with her prices. Though she still lives in KwaMashu, where she learned to weave from her neighbor Vusi Khanyile, her life is a far cry from those days in the restaurant.

opposite page, clockwise from top left:

**TURQUOISE PLATE WITH ANIMALS AND FIGURES**
Zama Khanyile
540 mm diameter
Collection of Melanie Cohen

**BLACK-AND-WHITE COWS**
Zama Khanyile
490 mm diameter
Private Collection

**RED PLATE WITH FIGURES AND HOUSES**
Zama Khanyile
540 mm diameter
Collection of David Arment

**LEOPARDS**
Zama Khanyile
400 mm diameter
Collection of David Arment

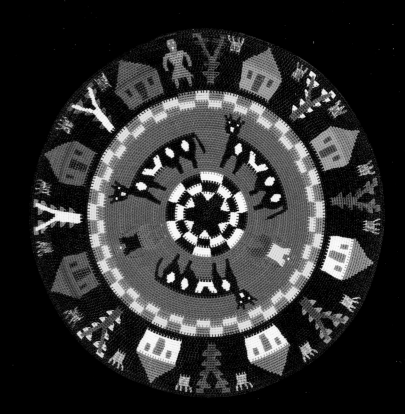

# MBONISENI KHANYILE

Born 1967, Eshowe

**M**boniseni is very independent, has a strong personality, and, like an archetypal artist, can be decidedly stubborn. He always arrives to sell his wares on the wrong day and he usually does so late on a Friday afternoon, when the buyers are tired and ready to go home. When questioned about his sense of timing, he remains unfazed, smiles or laughs, and simply continues the negotiation process. It's a skill he must have learned from a tough start in life.

In 1984 he left Emasunelwini High School in Eshowe, having completed only grade nine. This qualification did not get him very far, and he soon found himself working as a farm laborer, cutting sugar cane. With very little prospect of other work coming along, Mboniseni had no choice but to continue working as a laborer. He did so for eleven years until, in 1995, he decided to move to Durban in search of better pay. In Durban he found piece-work in the construction industry and as a cleaner.

In 1996 he moved to the more affordable settlement of Siyanda and began a new life in the midst of the Siyanda weavers. The move was life changing. Many of their neighbors were weaving for a living, and it was not long before his girlfriend, Bongiwe Doyisa, began learning to weave. She in turn taught him. He quickly learned how to make *izimbenge* (beer pot lids), and in 1997 he stopped doing piecework and began weaving full time. That same year he began supplying the BAT Shop.

Mboniseni says that the success of his neighbors Zodwa Maphumulo, Ntombifuthi Magwasa, and Simon Mavundla, was an inspiration to him, and that as he had excelled at craft at school, he felt he could be a success too.

Today he is known for his frog designs and for his brightly colored geometrics. He is skilled at including text in his designs, and as a result he has secured quite a number of commissions from collectors and the corporate sector. A number of his designs include AIDS slogans.

opposite page:
**ORANGE FROGS**
Mboniseni Khanyile
420 mm diameter
Private Collection

following pages, left:
**RED FROGS AND BUTTERFLIES**
Mboniseni Khanyile
410 mm diameter
Private Collection

following pages, right:
**AIDS KILLS**
Mboniseni Khanyile
390 mm diameter
Private Collection

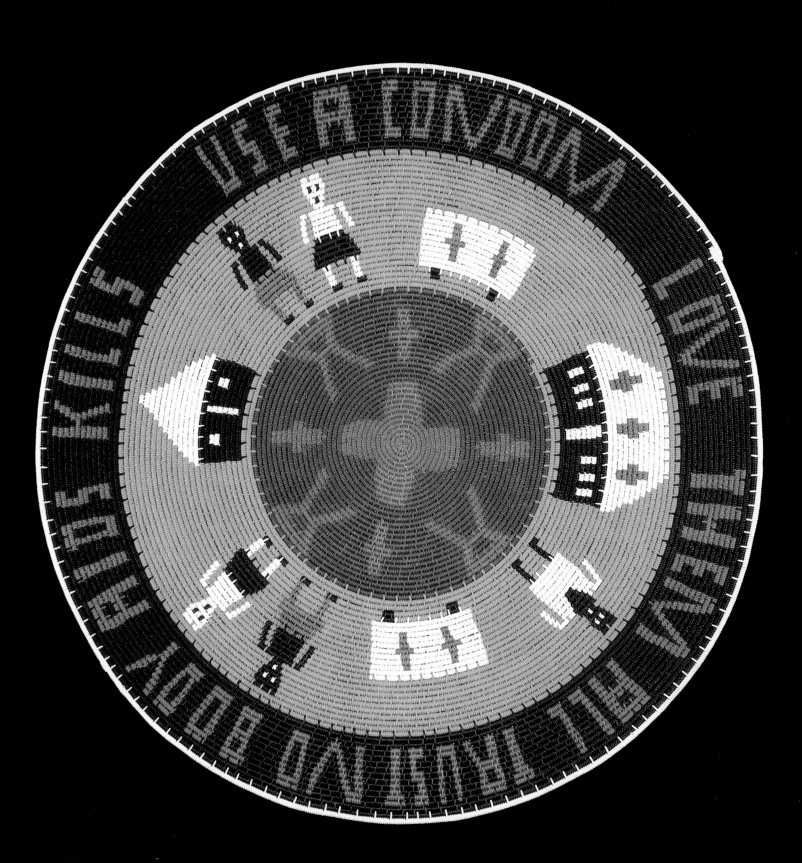

# NTOMBIFUTHI MAGWASA

Born 1965, Nongoma, KwaZulu-Natal

Ntombifuthi wove her first basket in 1993, after being taught how to weave by her neighbor Anamaria Dlamini in Siyanda. She had a natural talent for the craft and soon developed an unusually complex sense of color and balance in her designs. Inspired by the colors of the wire and how the colors work together, she experiments constantly with new patterns and scale. She looks for inspiration in books, magazines, and in the colors and patterns she sees around her. Her designs range from traditional Zulu patterns to bold contemporary patterns that reflect a melding of Zulu and Ndebele traditions.

Early on in her work Ntombifuthi displayed an exceptional talent. Marisa noted this at once and encouraged her to refine the shapes and sizes of her baskets and to develop her designs. Then Marisa lent her an embroidery book that included stunning designs on kelim carpets. Ntombifuthi was immediately interested in the complex patterns and designs. She kept the book for three months and returned with a basket showing the beginnings of her now-famous design style, a complex relationship of foreground to background.

In 1998 Ntombifuthi won the top prize in the prestigious FNB Vita Craft Now awards, South Africa's principal craft competition. The prize brought significant recognition for her and, by association, for all the telephone-wire weavers of Siyanda. Today she is an internationally recognized artist whose work is represented in many public and private collections locally and internationally.

But it was not all smooth sailing for Ntombifuthi. Like many South Africans, she has had her fair share of hardships. She was born in Nongoma into a conservative rural Zulu family, where her life was governed by set social, economic, and gender constraints. When she completed grade three, her father took her out of school and she was put to doing what is referred to as women's work. In the Magwasa family, she says, it was custom that girls did not go to school.

opposite page:
**LARGE OVAL ABSTRACT PLATE**
Ntombifuthi Magwasa
515 x 425 mm
Collection of David Arment

Luckily Ntombifuthi realized quite early that her lack of education was going to be a stumbling block in life. Influenced by her sister's skill at craft, and by economic necessity, she began a journey to find a means of making a living. The journey took her through a dressmaking course, into a milkshake flavor factory, and on into the world of telephone-wire basket weaving.

While living in Siyanda she met Bheki Sibiya, to whom she has taught the weaving technique. They are now married and have a family. Today the woman who once had never left her province, who once had never boarded a plane, describes herself as a businesswoman and a full-time artist. You may catch Ntombifuthi between baskets, at awards ceremonies and exhibitions, on flights to Cape Town and Chicago, Johannesburg and Perth, or simply enjoying her favorite curry at home in Durban.

opposite page:
**ABSTRACT PLATE**
Ntombifuthi Magwasa
450 mm diameter
Collection of Marisa Fick-Jordaan

following pages, left, clockwise from top left:
**ABSTRACT PLATE**
Ntombifuthi Magwasa
413 mm diameter
Private Collection

**ABSTRACT PLATE**
Ntombifuthi Magwasa
450 mm diameter
Collection of David Arment

**ABSTRACT PLATE**
Ntombifuthi Magwasa
440 mm diameter
Private Collection

**ABSTRACT PLATE**
Ntombifuthi Magwasa
476 mm diameter
Collection of David Arment

following pages, right, clockwise from top left:
**ABSTRACT PLATE**
Ntombifuthi Magwasa
370 mm diameter
Private Collection

**ABSTRACT PLATE**
Ntombifuthi Magwasa
375 mm diameter
Collection of Trisha Wilson

**ABSTRACT PLATE**
Ntombifuthi Magwasa
365 mm diameter
Collection of Marisa Fick-Jordaan

**ABSTRACT PLATE**
Ntombifuthi Magwasa
390 mm diameter
Collection of the Phansi Museum, Durban

# ROBERT MAJOLA

Born 1946, Eshowe, KwaZulu-Natal

Robert Majola traveled to Durban from the Eshowe area in 1982 looking for work. Unlike many other weavers, he did find employment and more than two decades later he is still working full time with Portnet, the National Port Authority, at the harbor in Durban. He produces baskets in his spare time.

Back in the early 1990s Robert noticed a fellow commuter from KwaMashu who spent his train journeys weaving objects from telephone wire. Fascinated by this occupation, Robert took informal lessons from the man during their daily trips. But the skill did not come easily; his tutor used an *usungulu* (a long needle) in his work, which Robert could not seem to master. Eventually, the man (whose name Robert does not know) let him use his hands, which is when, Robert says, everything started.

Since he began weaving, Robert, like many weavers, has collected his wire supplies from the scrap yards. The variety in his sources has influenced his use of colors, his palette ranging from primary to pastel colors, depending on what he can obtain. He does occasionally rely on formal suppliers for specific colors for special orders.

For molds he still uses the now-rusty, conventionally styled enamel bowls that he bought years ago from African trading stores in the rural areas. He works on these molds and has developed a unique soft-wire weave, creating small bowls with markedly geometric patterns. He creates between four and six pieces a week

He arrived at the BAT Shop soon after it opened in August 1995. Ever since then he has been a regular supplier, arriving to sell during his lunches, tea breaks, and on Saturdays. He jokes that he has to sneak away from work to deliver his bowls. That said, he is very proud of his success and has brought his boss and coworkers in to see that he really does sell his work at the BAT Shop.

opposite page, left to right:
**FOUR SOFT-WIRE BOWLS**
Robert Majola
140, 170, 140, and 170 mm diameter
Collection of Magda van der Vloed

# ZODWA MAPHUMULO

Born 1960, Port Shepstone, KwaZulu-Natal

Zodwa Maphumulo works as a full-time artist from her home in the settlement of Siyanda outside Durban. She was the first woman to learn telephone-wire basket weaving in 1992, and has since developed her weaving skills into a fine art. She enjoys local and international recognition and was chosen to represent South Africa at the Smithsonian Folk Art Festival in Washington, D.C., in 1999. Between 1998 and 2000 she worked on the Dirozulu project with the French artist Hervé Di Rosa. Visitors to the New Orleans Jazz Festival in 2004 were given the opportunity to meet her—she was one of twenty South African art crafters invited to attend and exhibit at the festival.

Zodwa's work is respected for a number of reasons. She is an expert weaver renowned for her high-quality baskets that include both geometric and figurative elements incorporating people and animals. She has developed unique elephant and dog characters, inspired by and adapted from the carpet designs she was shown. Her images of schoolgirls and of Zulu women have become her signature. Her form, too, is important: she has perfected a sophisticated and elegant shape for her plates, which have developed into a unique bowl structure. When it comes to color, she loves working with both pastels and brights but is particularly fond of pink, yellow, and purple.

Her success has taken her a long way. Born in 1960, she is the daughter of farm laborers. Like so many other children, she left school at an early age, having completed only grade six. She moved to Durban in 1980, at the age of twenty, and settled in KwaMashu, where she worked as a domestic servant for a black nurse. In 1984 she moved to Siyanda, built herself a shack, and took work as a domestic tog worker (a casual laborer) in neighboring Newlands East. She worked there from 1984 to 1992. Although life was still tough, the move to Siyanda was to be fortuitous.

At the settlement she encountered Bheki and Albert Dlamini, two of the handful of weavers at the time. Tired of poorly paid work, she spent time learning and developing her

opposite page:

**YELLOW BOWL WITH FIGURES**

Zodwa Maphumulo
470 mm diameter
Collection of David Arment

71

skill with Bheki and Albert. Bheki helped her find a market for her baskets through Paul Mikula, and in 1992 she left her job and began weaving full time. In 1995 Bheki introduced Zodwa to the BAT Shop. She laughs as she tells the story. Apparently Bheki dragged her and the four other Siyanda weavers down to the harbor by taxi from Siyanda. He had them traipsing under freeways, through the traffic, over railroad lines, and along the water's edge to find the shop. This was the start of a long relationship with Marisa and the BAT Shop, which continues to this day.

opposite page:
**COUPLES**
Zodwa Maphumulo
400 mm diameter
Collection of Marisa Fick-Jordaan

following pages, left, clockwise from top left:
**SCHOOL GIRLS**
Zodwa Maphumulo
408 mm diameter
Collection of David Arment

**BLACK CATS**
Zodwa Maphumulo
476 mm diameter
Private Collection

**PLATE WITH RED HEART**
Zodwa Maphumulo
370 mm diameter
Collection of Trisha Wilson

**RED, WHITE, AND BLUE SCHOOL GIRLS**
Zodwa Maphumulo
388 mm diameter
Collection of Oprah Winfrey

following pages, right:
**ZULU WOMEN**
Zodwa Maphumulo
420 mm diameter
Private Collection

# SIMON MAVUNDLA

### Born 1970, Kranskop, KwaZulu-Natal

Simon left school after completing grade nine, to earn a living. He started by making woodcarvings to sell within the Kranskop community, but in 1996 he moved to Siyanda and started looking for work in Durban. Fortunately he never found work. He did, however, meet his future wife, Nomvuselela Msimang, who taught him how to weave, and who introduced him to the BAT Shop.

In 1998 he completed a training course and began to emerge as a respected telephone-wire weaver. His skill was immediately evident and he was invited to work on the Dirozulu project. On that project, Simon worked closely with Hervé Di Rosa and this two-year interaction had a significant influence on Simon's use of color and form.

Complex weaving patterns define Simon's work, which contains a free-flowing style of geometric design incorporating plant and animal motifs. With the inclusion of snakes and eagles, he references aspects of Zulu mythology. In 2000 he received the Masibambane Award at an exhibition of contemporary Zulu baskets in Johannesburg, sponsored by the French Institute and the Alliance Française. This was his first visit to Johannesburg and a trip to the zoo there proved to be inspirational. It was after that that Simon first started adding animals to his geometric designs.

Simon's improved financial situation has allowed him to buy a bicycle and now he travels around Durban on his mountain bike, dressed for the Tour de France. One can only imagine this sporty figure, a lone cyclist in a world of crammed taxis, weaving through the traffic and flying past the pedestrians and bus queues, with his latest creation safely tucked into his backpack. House proud, he has painted his tin home a royal blue that stands out from the other homes, and has a neat fenced garden in the front.

With demand for his baskets growing, Simon was eventually able to afford the last down payment of his *lobola,* the traditional price for a bride in Zulu culture. He and Nomvuselela were married at the end of 2003.

opposite page:
**CROCODILES AND SNAKE**
Simon Mavundla
440 mm diameter
Collection of David Arment

following pages, left:
**CRABS AND EAGLES**
Simon Mavundla
432 mm diameter
Private Collection

following pages, right:
**SNAKES AND BIRDS**
Simon Mavundla
425 mm diameter
Collection of David Arment

# ELLIOT MKHIZE

Born 1945, Richmond, KwaZulu-Natal

Elliot was introduced to the world of weaving at a young age, when he went to school at Inhlazuka near Richmond. At school, children in the early grades were taught grass-weaving techniques in their art-and-craft classes. At the same time he was introduced to art and, one could say, to the economy of art at home, where both his grandfather and his father carved wooden spoons and utensils for trading. Using money he earned from his craftwork, his grandfather was even able to buy cattle for *lobola*. So in the 1960s, when Elliot had to choose a career path, it seemed natural that he chose to study at the reputable Ndaleni Art School in Richmond, which was then enjoying its heyday.

But, art being art and economic reality its often ugly self, Elliot went back to Sibonelo High School to finish his formal education. Thereafter, he found a job as a supervisor with Lever Brothers in Durban. In 1968 his daughter, the first of ten children, was born. From then on, his growing family necessitated steady employment and Elliot stayed on with Lever Brothers for several years. Then followed a brief stint as a machine operator at the *Natal Mercury* newspaper. A job at the Natal Playhouse theater as a night watchman was his brush with destiny. He was introduced to the "night watchman's art," the world of telephone-wire weaving.

After observing his fellow night watchmen use wire to decorate the handles of their sticks, Elliot began to experiment with telephone wire. He, however, worked with the more traditional bowl form and, in so doing, became one of the originators of the contemporary form of coiled-wire baskets. He wove his first basket in 1973, and took it to the African Art Centre in Durban. Jo Thorpe snapped it up and put it into the African Art Centre's collection, where it was displayed in the shop until it was stolen in a robbery. Elliot quickly became a sought-after weaver and in 1984 he began working full time as an artist. He is currently South Africa's most renowned and successful telephone-wire weaver, and the only master weaver with formal art school training.

opposite page:
**ABSTRACT PLATE**
Elliot Mkhize
360 mm diameter
Collection of David Arment

In one of his first works, Elliot used traditional designs, and included his name in prominent letters. Today he is known for his highly developed sense of color, weaving quality, and design detail. He typically uses abstract patterns, with occasional figures or letters, usually his initials, and he is a master at weaving intricate patterns in black and white. His trademark is an extremely tight weave, which gives his baskets a weight and density unlike any others.

Elliot was one of the first weavers to travel abroad, and has been to America, Denmark, France, Namibia, and Sweden. In 1995 he won a merit award in the FNB Vita Craft Now competition. He is also represented in major South African and international collections of contemporary Zulu arts. In the past he has been contracted to run workshops for weavers at the BAT Centre, and at the Durban Art Gallery he occasionally runs classes for hobby crafters.

opposite page, clockwise from top left:
**ABSTRACT PLATE**
Elliot Mkhize
255 mm diameter
Private Collection

**ABSTRACT PLATE**
Elliot Mkhize
273 mm diameter
Private Collection

**ABSTRACT PLATE**
Elliot Mkhize
290 mm diameter
Private Collection

**ABSTRACT PLATE**
Elliot Mkhize
280 mm diameter
Collection of the Phansi Museum, Durban

following pages, left:
**ABSTRACT PLATE**
Elliot Mkhize
280 mm diameter
Collection of Marisa Fick-Jordaan

following pages, right:
**ABSTRACT PLATE**
Elliot Mkhize
320 x 290 mm
Collection of the Phansi Museum, Durban

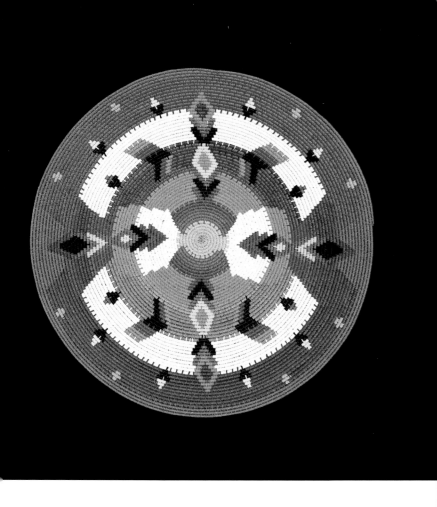

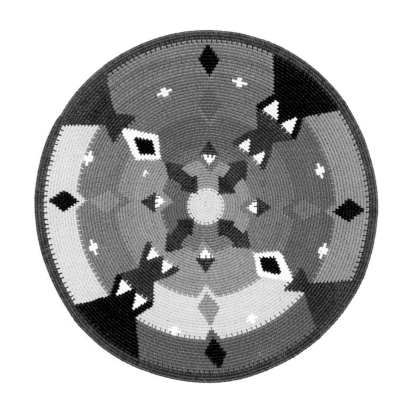

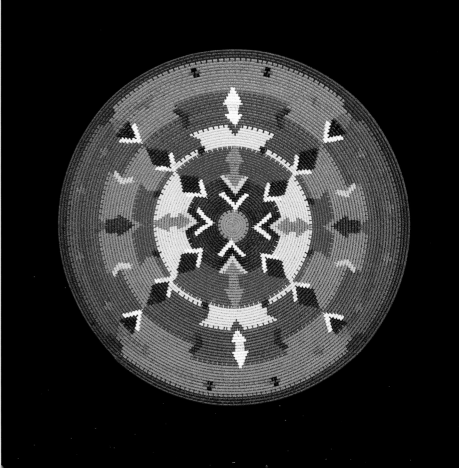

# JAHENI MKHIZE

Born 1953, Greytown, KwaZulu-Natal

An accomplished weaver, Jaheni Mkhize is a consistent supplier to the BAT Shop. The quality of her work is exceptional and is frequently accepted for the FNB Vita Craft Now competitions

Jaheni uses the soft-wire technique that is the basis of much of the BAT Shop's zenzulu collection. Her weaving is done over a mold and on a scale that is unusually large. A perfectionist who weaves flawless baskets of outstanding quality, she loves working with vibrant colors. Yet she is also a natural minimalist, a quality that works well with soft-wire contemporary forms.

In Zulu culture a child's name always has a significant, and often literal, meaning. The Zulu word *jaha* means to chase, gallop, race, or be in a hurry. Her name refers to how quickly she was born and its meaning remains appropriate: she is a prolific weaver and learns, absorbs, and incorporates new ideas very quickly. She adapts and experiments frequently, and shows heaps of initiative, always seeking to take her craft and design forward.

Jaheni was first introduced to the world of wire weaving by her friend Mbopiseni Ngubani, one of the Waayhoek weavers. Mbopiseni used to visit Jaheni in Greytown, and taught her the craft during these visits. At that stage Jaheni pursued weaving as a hobby. In 1995 she moved to Siyanda in search of a place of her own. There she took further weaving lessons from Elliot Ndwandwe, the unofficial chief of the settlement. During that time she made four coiled baskets and sold them to the BAT Shop. Growing in confidence, she produced a soft-wire basket to sell. That single basket led to the later development of what became known as the Jaheni range of small bowls.

In addition to weaving, Jaheni was employed to teach the soft-wire technique at a BAT Shop workshop. Several members of her family attended the workshop, some coming all the way from Greytown. Her family remains the core group of zenzulu weavers.

opposite page:
**RED-AND-PURPLE ZIGZAG BOWL**
Jaheni Mkhize
380 mm diameter
Collection of David Arment

following pages, left:
**LARGE, BRIGHT BOWL**
Jaheni Mkhize
275 x 350 mm
Collection of David Arment

following pages, right:
**ZIGZAG LAMPSHADE BOWL**
Jaheni Mkhize
380 mm diameter
Private Collection

# ALFRED NTULI

Born 1953, Maphumulo, KwaZulu-Natal

In 1985 Alfred moved to KwaMashu in Durban from the Maphumulo region of rural KwaZulu-Natal. A year later his family joined him and they moved to Siyanda, where they settled next door to Bheki Dlamini. This move was a turning point for Alfred as Bheki exposed him to the craft of telephone-wire weaving and he quickly set about weaving himself. Rather than weaving the same form as Bheki favored, Alfred wove vessels based on the shape of the *izinkhamba* (round beer pots), for which he later developed lids with an embedded top. Most of the weavers today still weave *izimbenge* (beer pot lids), and so Alfred's *izinkhamba* have become his trademark.

Alfred says that he learned the basics of weaving simply by watching Bheki work, but that Bheki actively taught him how to incorporate designs into the weaving process. In terms of design, he was originally inspired by the designs and colors used in traditional Maphumulo beadwork, but today he uses a wide palette of colors.

Between 1986 and 1987 he sold his work to other Siyanda residents who resold his work in Durban, but in 1987 Bheki introduced him to Paul Mikula and to the African Art Centre, where he started selling his creations more commercially. Paul became an active collector of Alfred's pots, is still Alfred's first sales stop today, and Paul's collection, housed at the Phansi Museum, includes a large collection of Alfred's work.

In 2000 Alfred and his family moved back to Maphumulo and into his original family homestead. His success today enables him to travel from there to Durban to sell his wares.

opposite page:
**ABSTRACT LIDDED POT**
Alfred Ntuli
215 x 254 mm
Collection of David Arment

following pages, left:
**YELLOW LIDDED POT**
Alfred Ntuli
190 x 230 mm
Collection of David Arment

following pages, right:
**THREE LIDDED POTS**
Alfred Ntuli
230 x 250, 225 x 240, and 215 x 240 mm
Collection of the Phansi Museum, Durban

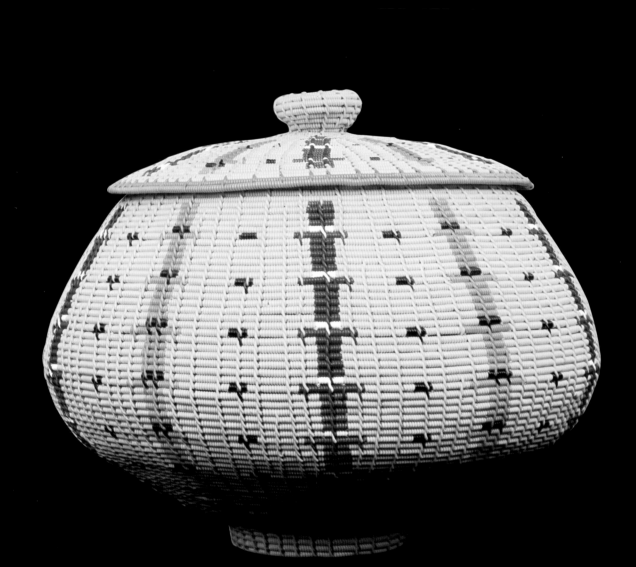

# BHEKI SIBIYA

Born 1955, Hlabisa, KwaZulu-Natal

Bheki is married to Ntombifuthi Magwasa, who taught him how to weave. As a result of his and of his wife's success with their baskets, Bheki has recently stopped working at odd jobs and is focusing exclusively on his weaving.

He frequently collaborates with Ntombifuthi on design and pattern, and the influence is often apparent in their work. Yet the addition of stripes, diagonal patterns, and zigzags is what distinguishes his work. He identifies pink, red, purple, turquoise, and silver as his favorite colors. Bheki enjoys the challenge presented by the complexity of new design interpretations, but continues to find inspiration in traditional geometric Zulu beadwork patterns from the Nongoma and Hlabisa districts.

He comes from Hlabisa, a region that specializes in the making of traditional Zulu grass baskets. Although his mother made woven sleeping mats for practical use, there was no history of craft making in his immediate family. Perhaps this is why he lined his first wire *ukhamba* (clay beer pot) with thick glue, so that it would hold water and thus be more useful. Because the other weavers were producing *imbenge*, he initially produced a few *ukhamba* vessels with lids, hoping to corner a new market. Later he realized that large-scale *imbenge*-shaped baskets would have better financial returns as they appeal to collectors, a more lucrative market.

In 1973 Bheki arrived in Durban, where he managed to find odd jobs as a plumber and gardener. He relocated to Siyanda in 1988, where he met Ntombifuthi. Breaking with patriarchal tradition, Bheki supports Ntombifuthi's new-found fame and travels, and is happy to stay at home to look after the children and keep the home fires burning.

opposite page:
**LARGE, OVAL ABSTRACT PLATE**
Bheki Sibiya
460 x 380 mm
Collection of David Arment

# VINCENT SITHOLE

Born 1970, Ilenge, Ladysmith,
KwaZulu-Natal

Tired of pushing wheelbarrows on construction sites in Ladysmith, Vincent Sithole moved temporarily to Siyanda in 1996 and lived with his sister while scouting for work. He failed to find any useful employment, but luckily discovered the vibrant Siyanda telephone-wire weaving community right under his nose.

First he noticed Bheki Dlamini weaving, and then others. He watched them and taught himself the technique. His first basket was monochromatic, but he soon produced work that showed a flair for pattern and color. Albert Dlamini, who helped him find materials, also introduced him to the BAT Shop. His early work showed his exceptional talent, and Marisa began buying his baskets immediately. Since establishing a name for himself, Vincent has moved back to his rural home outside Ladysmith, where he works and lives with his family.

Vincent's intricate geometric patterning and unusual combinations of color created designs reminiscent of stained-glass windows. He also references the natural environment, incorporating images of birds and plants into his designs. His interest in nature began, he says, as a child, when he used to herd his father's cattle and watching and interacting with the animals kept him occupied through the long hours. Vincent also enjoyed observing snakes, birds, and insects, the fish in the iThukela River and, more recently, the monkeys he saw while living in Siyanda. Incorporating these images in his work takes him back to his childhood.

In 1998 Vincent participated on the Dirozulu project. Hervé Di Rosa's designs called on him to weave in a free-flowing, figurative style, very different from the geometric patterns of his own work. The increased scale, bands of color, and organic shapes of Di Rosa's designs have had a lasting influence on Vincent's work. Large-scale pieces, such as *Zulu Wedding*, in the collection of the Mpumalanga Provincial Legislature, and *Bugs*, which is in David Arment's collection, express his increasing confidence and imaginative use of figurative and geometric designs.

opposite page:
**CIRCLE OF LIFE**
Vincent Sithole
560 mm diameter
Collection of David Arment

The story behind *Nature*, which is in Marisa Fick-Jordaan's collection, is quite beautiful. In 2002 Vincent's childhood home burned down and the family lost everything. After the fire they rebuilt the home and Vincent produced the basket titled *Nature*. The design is filled with images from nature and symbolically deals with the Creation and renewal.

In 1999 Vincent won first prize in the BAT Shop Masibambane Trust telephone-wire weaving competition. This prize led to his being invited to travel to Australia in 2000, one of the guest artists at the Durbs to *Freo Wire and Metal Act* exhibition, presented at the Perth International Arts Festival. Vincent's work has always been selected for the FNB Vita Craft Now Awards, and in 2003 he won the gold award. Most recently he was invited to exhibit his work at the inaugural Santa Fe International Folk Art Market in July 2004.

opposite page:

**GARDEN**

Vincent Sithole

600 mm diameter, Collection of Marisa Fick-Jordaan

following pages, left, clockwise from top left:

**BROWN SNAKES AND WHITE DUCKS**

Vincent Sithole

530 mm diameter, Collection of Trisha Wilson

**BLACK MAMBA**

Vincent Sithole

394 mm diameter, Private Collection

**STAINED-GLASS PATTERN IN RINGS**

Vincent Sithole

310 mm diameter, Private Collection

**BUTTERFLIES**

Vincent Sithole

390 mm diameter, Private Collection

following pages, right, clockwise from top left:

**TWO LIONS**

Vincent Sithole

340 mm diameter, Collection of David Arment

**STAINED-GLASS PATTERN**

Vincent Sithole

305 mm diameter, Collection of David Arment

**RHINOS**

Vincent Sithole

420 mm diameter, Private Collection

**BUGS AND A SNAKE, PATTERNED AFTER A GIFT WRAP DESIGN**

Vincent Sithole

650 mm diameter, Collection of David Arment

page 102:

**BLACK CHAMELEONS WITH FLOWERS**

Vincent Sithole

465 mm diameter, Collection of Margaret Daniel

page 103:

**THREE ZULU DANCERS**

Vincent Sithole

546 mm diameter, Collection of David Arment

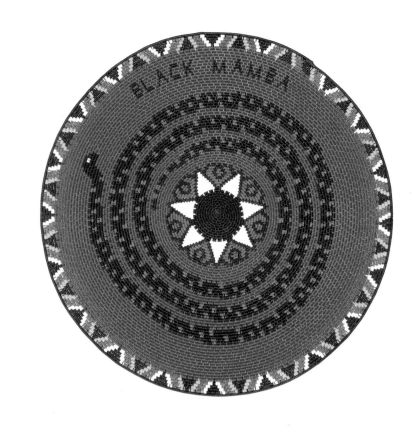

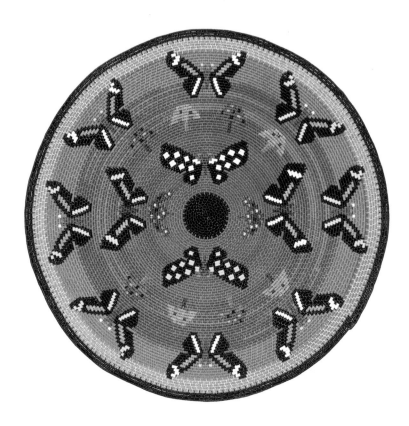

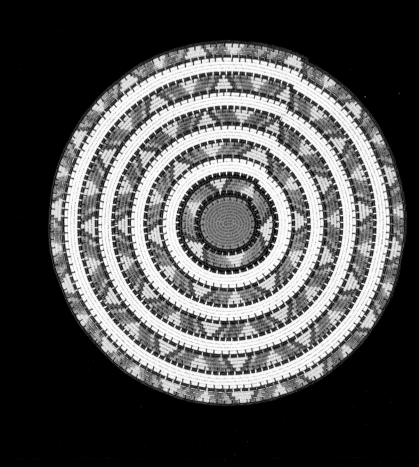

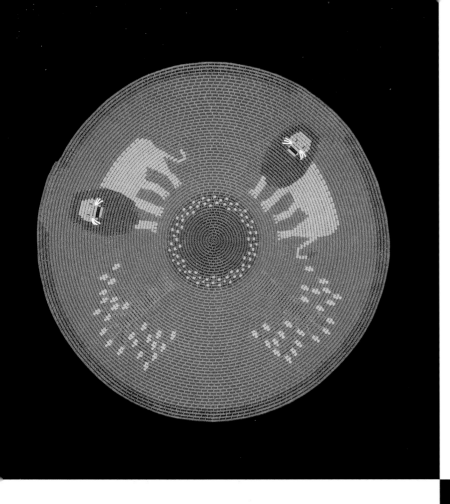

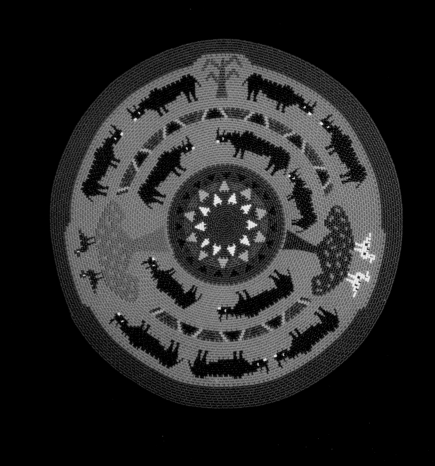

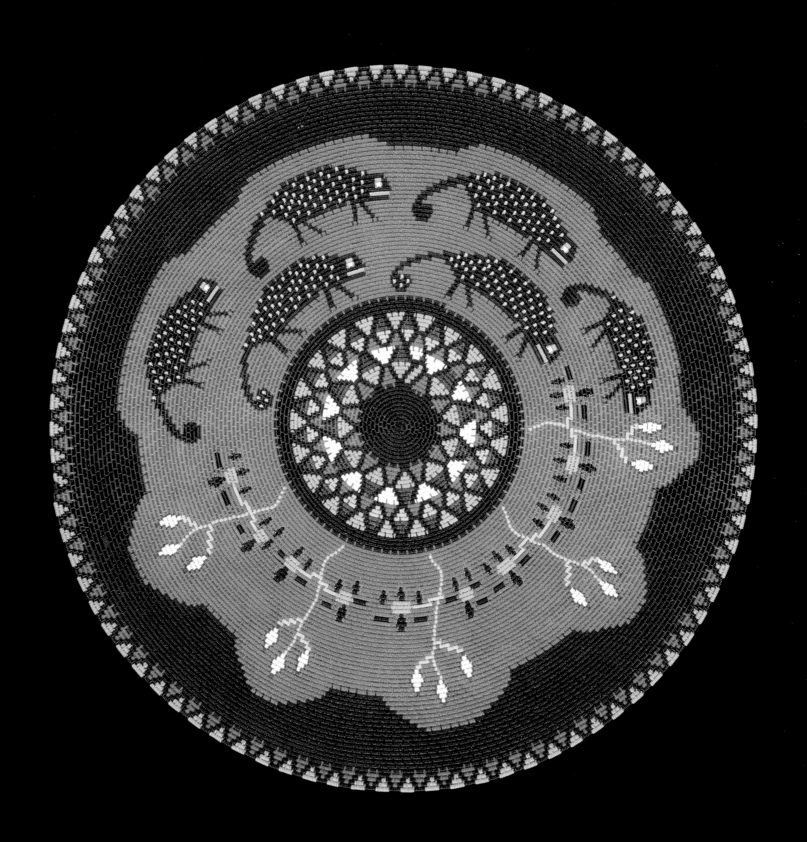

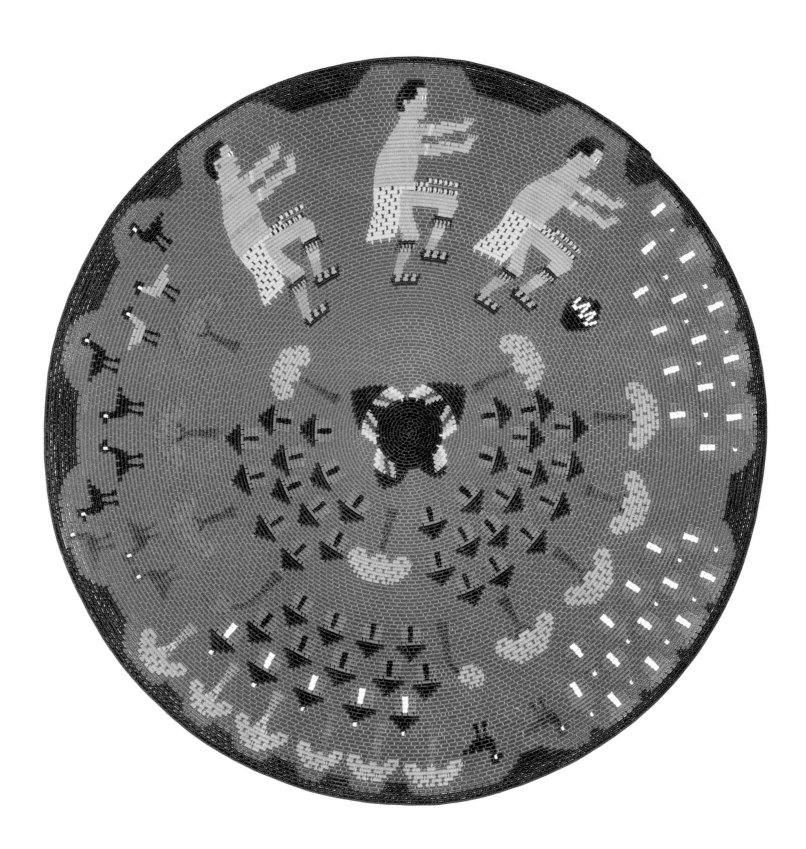

# COLLECTIONS 3

The world has become a very small place. The early baskets traveled no further than to local collections in Durban; now the baskets are in collections all over the world. Through the marketing activities of the BAT Shop in Durban, stores in Paris, New York, Los Angeles, and London carry these baskets. International designers discovered in them an easy way to add an African touch to design projects. The Design Museum in London featured the baskets in an exhibit, and periodicals from *Elle Décor* to *Vogue* have included the baskets on covers as well as in their sections on hot trends.

Collectors have found the baskets irresistible, and collecting the wire plates can become addictive. A few collectors have become nothing short of passionate about them, citing, variously, the attraction of the colors, the artists, the designs, and the shapes. Dedicated collectors have found that one or two were simply not enough. What they wanted was to have baskets from all of the best weavers. Some collectors have focused on a specific style, a specific color palette (such as monochromatic or black-and-white baskets), a specific type of design (such the inclusion of figures or animals), a specific cultural motif (such as the AIDS epidemic); others are attracted to the contemporary styles of zenzulu; yet oth-

opposite page:
**PRIVATE RESIDENCE**
Santa Fe, New Mexico
Plate with copper wire over electrical wire
Artist unknown
*Photograph by Peter Vitale*

ers, and these are in the majority, have broader interests, and decline to limit the scope of their collections.

Telephone-wire baskets have a sophisticated aesthetic, contemporary yet very African, colorful, and distinctive. African art has long been a fundamental complement to contemporary art. The primitivism movement established the link between artifacts from Africa and contemporary art design. The baskets are entirely at home in a contemporary environment. That said, the baskets are not out of place elsewhere. The integration of craft into design can lend a more traditional aesthetic in a funky eclectic design; and these baskets can even become part of a collection of art in a traditional environment.

opposite page:
**PRIVATE RESIDENCE**
Durban, South Africa
*Photograph by Sally Chance*

following pages, left and right:
**PRIVATE RESIDENCE**
Dallas, Texas

AFRICAN CEREMONIES

AFRICAN CEREMONIES

opposite page:

**PRIVATE RESIDENCE**

Santa Fe, New Mexico

*Photograph by Peter Vitale*


previous pages, left:

**HOME OF SUSAN AND VANCE CAMPBELL**

Santa Fe, New Mexico

*Photograph by Peter Vitale*


previous pages, right:

**PRIVATE RESIDENCE**

Santa Fe, New Mexico

*Photograph by Peter Vitale*

PLATES.

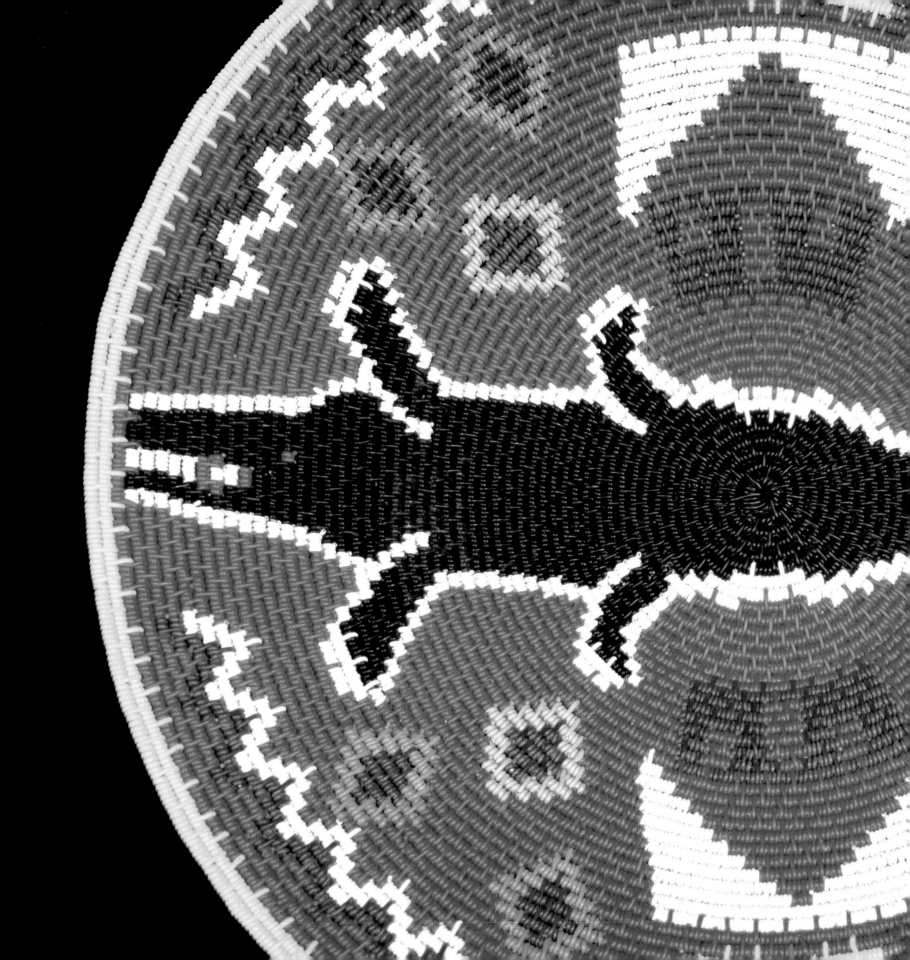

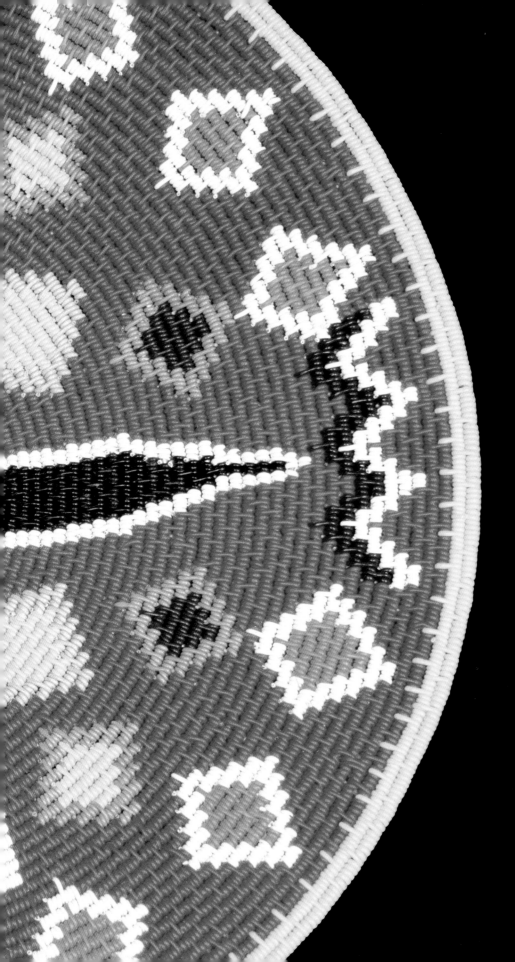

Basket weaving has a long tradition in African cultures. The transformation of available materials into useful objects is an art of utility. The introduction of telephone wire and, later, the availability of a stable supply of material in a wide range of colors, had a profound effect on the Zulu basket weavers. These colors immediately and dramatically opened the possibility of elevating this craft into art. Since the introduction of telephone wire, the colors have inspired many uses. The decoration of everyday objects, such as bottles, and ceremonial pieces, such as dancing sticks, has become more brilliant with the complex patterning that is possible with the colors that are now available.

Traditions and contemporary design fuse. From the traditional to the contemporary, telephone-wire baskets tell us stories and delight us with their complex and diverse pattern and detail. The sources of these contemporary patterns, clearly apparent in the baskets, include Zulu mythology, beadwork patterns, basketry designs, fabric and dress patterns, and houses of all shapes and sizes.

The objects illustrated here present an overview of the history and development of the use of wire. The designs often reflect an immediacy of personal experience, and are thus the stuff of life: people, celebrities, events, sports, nature, urban and rural landscapes, forms of transport, and traditional symbols.

opposite:
**CROCODILE PLATE**
Busi Ndlovu
280 mm diameter
Collection of David Arment

previous pages, left:
**BLACK AND WHITE ABSTRACT PLATE**
Joyce Mkhize
298 mm diameter
Private Collection

## ZIGZAGS

One of the patterns evident in the earliest telephone-wire baskets is the zigzag. This pattern is also the most prevalent in the coverings on bottles and sticks and, since the 1980s, in the soft-wire bowls made first in the Waayhoek project and later developed into small nests of baskets in various color combinations by the BAT Shop. The zigzag also appears on early telephone-wire *izimbenge* and in the cladding, with telephone wire, of the traditional Zulu basket made from *ilala* palm—this is done to keep the rats out, a functional rather than a decorative application although the end result belies this.

opposite page:
**TRADITIONAL *ILALA* PALM BASKET**
**COVERED IN TELEPHONE WIRE**
**(TO KEEP THE RATS OUT)**
Artist unknown
360 x 360 mm
Private Collection

**TELEPHONE-WIRE BOWL**
Artist unknown
175 x 50 mm
Collection of Marisa Fick-Jordaan

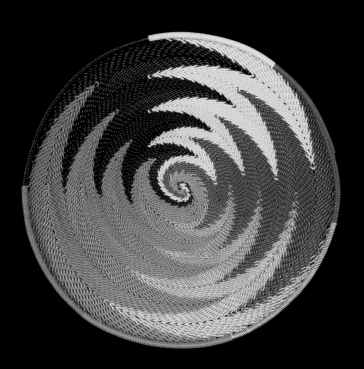

**TELEPHONE-WIRE BOWL**
Artist unknown
190 x 50 mm
Collection of Marisa Fick-Jordaan

opposite page:
**THREE BRIGHT BOWLS**
Robert Majola
180, 150, 100 mm diameter
Collection of Marisa Fick-Jordaan

**TWO TELEPHONE-WIRE BAGS**
190 x 120 x 50 mm
Collection of Marisa Fick-Jordaan

**GLASS JAR COVERED IN TELEPHONE WIRE**
Artist unknown
260 x 160 mm
Collection of Marisa Fick-Jordaan

opposite page:
**ZIGZAG BOWL**
Sipjo Khuzwop
280 mm diameter
Collection of David Arment

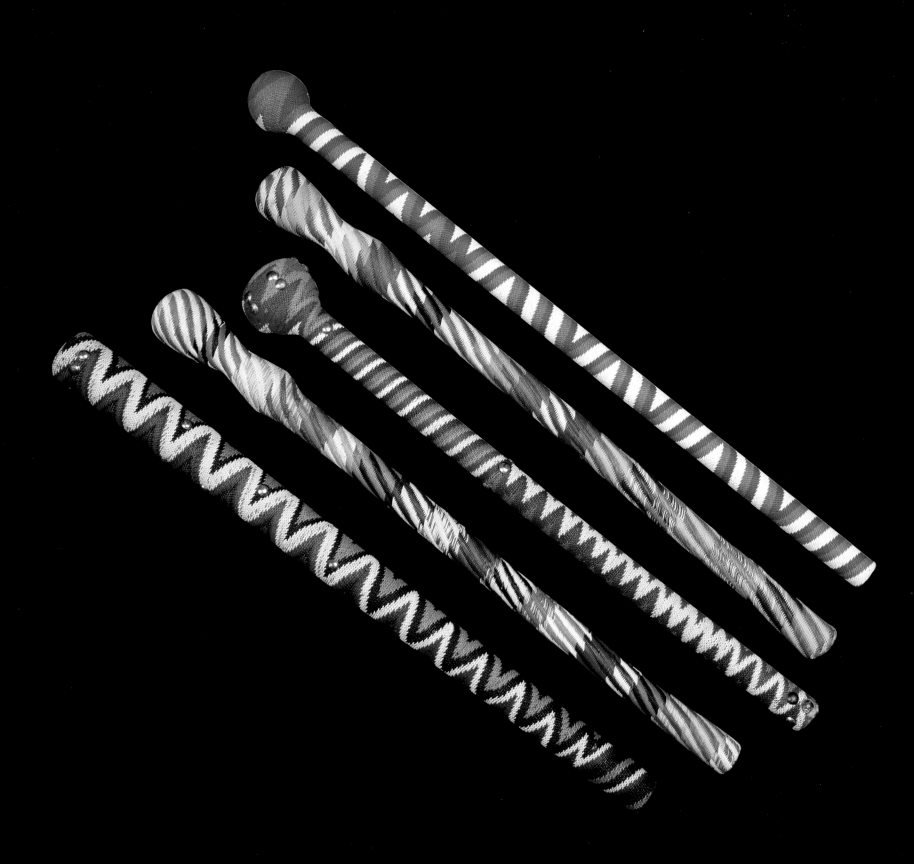

**GLASS BOTTLES COVERED IN TELEPHONE WIRE**
Artist unknown (left)
Sduduzi Gabela (center and right)
h: 320, 255, 285 mm
Private Collection

previous pages, left:
**FIVE WOODEN STICKS COVERED IN TELEPHONE WIRE**
Artists unknown, 20th century
top to bottom, h: 570, 530, 510, 530, 530 mm
Collection of David Arment

previous pages, right:
**TWO WOODEN STICKS COVERED IN TELEPHONE WIRE WITH METAL STUDS**
Artists unknown, 20th Century
h: 530, 510 mm
Collection of David Arment

**GLASS BOTTLES COVERED IN TELEPHONE WIRE**
Sduduzi Gabela
h: 320, 235 mm
Private Collection

opposite page:
**GLASS BOTTLES COVERED IN TELEPHONE WIRE**
Artists unknown
h: 265, 180, 460, 215, 265 mm
Private Collection

**GLASS BOTTLE COVERED IN TELEPHONE WIRE**
Artist unknown
h: 320 mm
Private Collection

**GLASS BOTTLE COVERED IN TELEPHONE WIRE**
Artist unknown
h: 220 mm
Collection of Marisa Fick-Jordaan

opposite page:
**TELEPHONE-WIRE COFFEE POT**
Alfred Ntuli
220 x 180 mm
Collection of the Phansi Museum, Durban

**TELEPHONE-WIRE TEA SERVICE**
Artist unknown
Campbell Collections, Durban

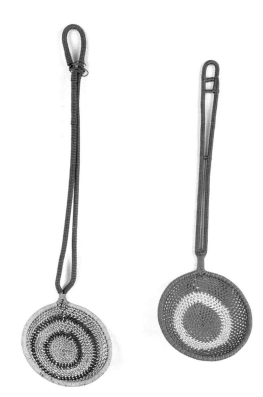

*ISIKHETHO* **(BEER STRAINERS)**
Artists unknown
h: 320, 270 mm
Collection of the Phansi Museum, Durban

*ISIKHETHO* **(BEER STRAINERS)**
Artists unknown
h: 330, 270, 350 mm
Collection of Marisa Fick-Jordaan

opposite page:
**KITCHEN KNIVES WITH TELEPHONE-WIRE-COVERED HANDLES**
Amos Khubisa
h: 170, 205, 170, 205, 260 mm
Private Collection

**TELEPHONE-WIRE VASE**
Alfred Ntuli
178 x 165 mm
Private Collection

**TWO LIDDED POTS**
Alfred Ntuli
205 x 205 and 190 x 190 mm
Private Collection

opposite page:
**ORANGE LIDDED POT**
Mr. B. W. Gcaba
152 x 228 mm
Collection of David Arment

**TWO BOWLS**
Artists unknown
270 x 105 and 220 x 60 mm
Collection of Marisa Fick-Jordaan

**TWO PLASTIC SALAD BOWLS COVERED WITH TELEPHONE WIRE**
Themba Ndlovu
255 x 210 x 100 and 350 x 210 x 100 mm
Collection of Marianne Fassler

opposite page:
**TELEPHONE-WIRE POT AND BOWL**
Pot by Siyanaphi Shangase
216 x 228 mm
Bowl by Gideon Nzuza
310 mm
Private Collection

136

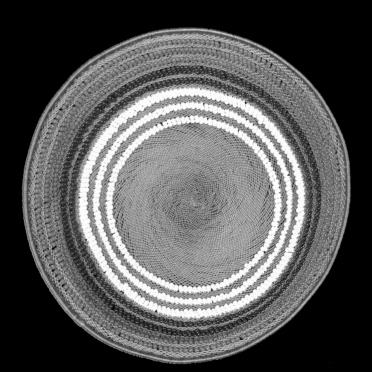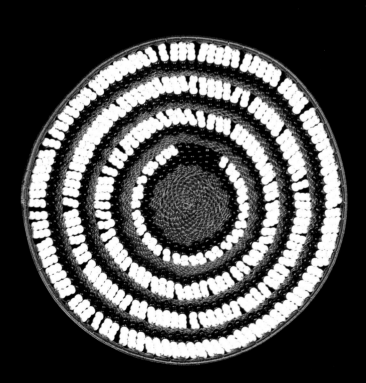

## SWIRLS

Another pattern seen in early telephone-wire baskets is the swirl. This pattern is also found in soft-wire bowls, for which the shape is made over a form. Soft-wire baskets started showing up in the 1980s in funky color combinations that were the result of the limited availability of wire.

opposite page:

**ZENZULU BOWLS**

150, 150, and 190 mm diameter

Private Collection

previous pages, left, clockwise from top left:

**COPPER BOWL WITH BLACK AND WHITE BEADS**

Artist unknown

197 mm diameter

Private Collection

**COPPER BOWL WITH GLASS BEADS**

Artist unknown

210 mm diameter

Private Collection

**COPPER BOWL WITH BLACK AND WHITE BEADS**

Artist unknown

210 mm diameter

Private Collection

**COPPER BOWL WITH BLUE AND WHITE GLASS BEADS**

Artist unknown

203 mm diameter

Private Collection

previous pages, right:

**ZENZULU LAMPSHADE WITH COPPER-WIRE**

**AND GLASS-BEADED EGGS**

Artists unknown

380 mm diameter

Private Collection

**ZENZULU BOWL**
190 mm diameter
Private Collection

**ZENZULU BOWL**
190 mm diameter
Private Collection

opposite page:
**THREE BLACK BOWLS WITH A WHITE SWIRL**
Artist unknown
152, 195, and 254 mm diameter
Private Collection

opposite page, clockwise from top left:

**PURPLE AND GREEN BOWL**
Linus Ngube
178 mm
Private Collection

**BLACK-AND-WHITE ZIGZAG BOWL**
Artist unknown
190 mm
Private Collection

**PURPLE AND BLUE BOWL**
Linus Ngube
178 mm
Private Collection

**BLACK-AND-WHITE ZIGZAG BOWL**
Artist unknown
190 mm
Private Collection

following pages, left:
**ZENZULU BOWL**
190 mm
Private Collection

following pages, right:
**STACKED ZENZULU BOWLS**
190 mm each
Private Collection

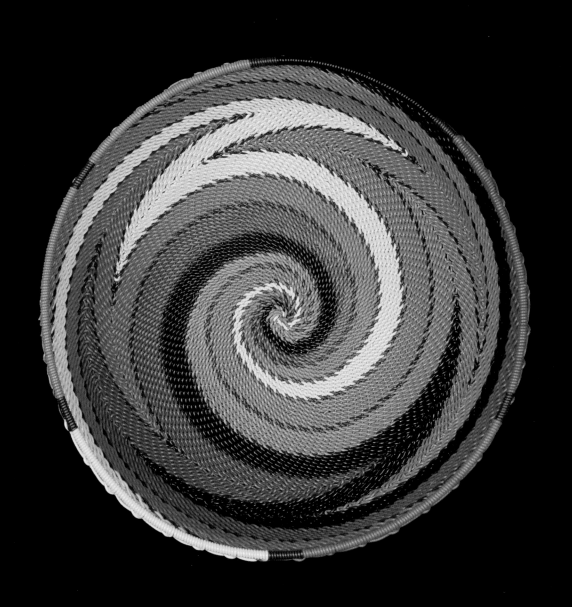

## ZULU FLOWERS

What we call the Zulu Flower (*imbali*) is one of the original patterns used in telephone-wire baskets and is based on traditional patterns used for grass and palm *izimbenge*. This simple stylized design—a naïve rendition of a circle with petals radiating from the center—is, however, not confined to Zulu expression, and can be seen in coiled baskets of other regions of the world, including American Indians. The pattern lends itself to the circular form of basketry and appears in endless variations, sometimes quite elaborate. The first exhibitions at the BAT Centre were full of small-scale baskets decorated with variations of this pattern. With the growing confidence of the artists, this floral motif has become increasingly complex, a development that may be seen in a comparison of the earlier work of Bheki Dlamini with the later work of Ntombifuthi Magwasa and Simon Mavundla.

**PLATES WITH ZULU FLOWER PATTERN**
Various artists and sizes
Collection of Marisa Fick-Jordaan and
The Phansi Museum, Durban

following page left and right:
**BLUE ZULU FLOWER PLATE**
Artist unknown
250 x 225 mm, Collection of Marisa Fick-Jordaan

**ZULU FLOWER PLATE**
Artist unknown
250 mm diameter, Collection of Marisa Fick-Jordaan

**GREEN ZULU FLOWER PLATE**
Artist unknown
255 mm diameter, Collection of Marisa Fick-Jordaan

**BOWL WITH ZULU FLOWER PATTERN**
Bheki Dlamini
130 mm diameter, Collection of Marisa Fick-Jordaan

**ZULU FLOWER ABSTRACTION**
Nomthandazo Mtikitiki
406 mm diameter, Collection of David Arment

**ZULU FLOWER PLATE**
Busisiwe Makhanya
250 mm diameter, Private Collection

**PLATE WITH ZULU FLOWER**
Nomthandazo Mtikitiki
400 mm diameter, Collection of the Phansi Museum, Durban

**ZULU FLOWER PLATE**
Busisiwe Makhanya
260 mm diameter, Private Collection

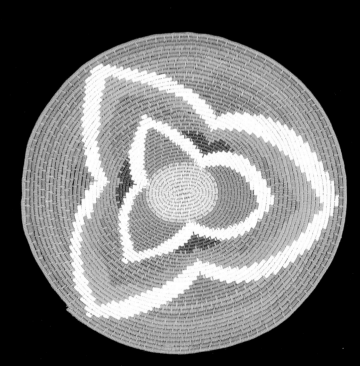

## SPORTS

Sports have always been an important part of South African life and, since 1994, national soccer, rugby, and cricket events have brought many South Africans together. In 1995 South Africa hosted and won the Rugby World Cup, and in 1996 hosted and won the Africa Nations Cup for soccer. The excitement of these events inspired a series of baskets celebrating the national teams and events. "Bafana Bafana," the Zulu name for the South African soccer team, appears often on plates. Those baskets were the precursors to a series of rugby and soccer World Cup baskets that have honored the winners of these events, such as Australia and France.

**BAFANA BAFANA WITH LOOPED CUT-OUT**
Dudu Cele
315 mm diameter
Collection of Marisa Fick-Jordaan

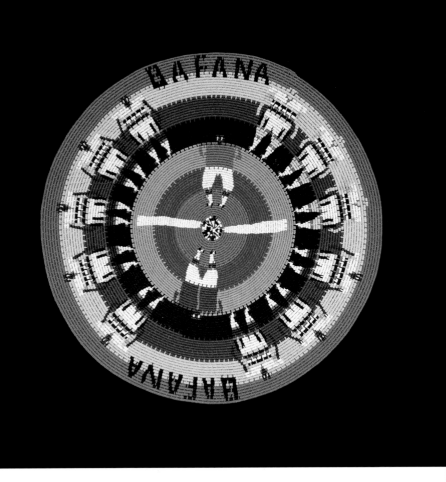

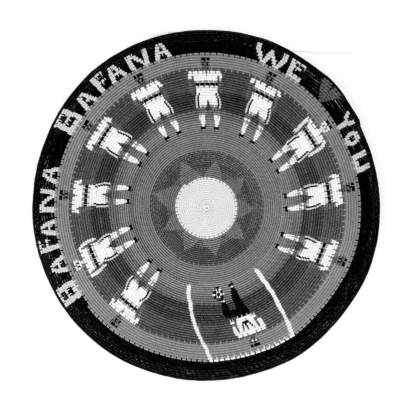

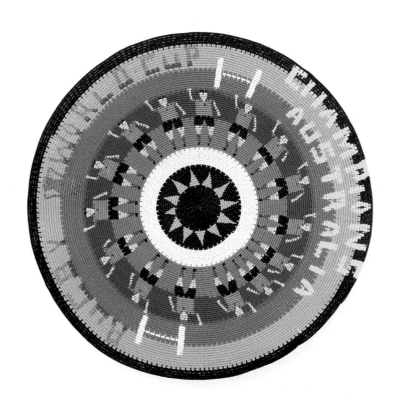

top left:
**SPRINGBOK RUGBY W--- CUP**
Bheki Dlamini
320 mm diameter
Collection of Marisa Fick-Jordaan

bottom left:
**BAFANA BAFANA 1996**
Bheki Dlamini
340 mm diameter
Collection of Marisa Fick-Jordaan

opposite page, clockwise from top left:
**BAFANA BAFANA**
Dudu Celi
394 mm diameter
Private Collection

**BAFANA BAFANA WE LOVE YOU**
Dudu Celi
370 mm diameter
Collection of David Arment

**BAFANA BAFANA FRANCE 98**
Bheki Dlamini
400 mm diameter
Collection of Marisa Fick-Jordaan

**RUGBY WORLD CUP CHAMPIONS AUSTRALIA**
Bheki Dlamini
432 mm diameter
Collection of David Arment

## NEW SOUTH AFRICA

The formal end of the apartheid system of government in 1994 resulted in a wave of national pride.
Nelson Mandela and the new flag became important
themes for the telephone-wire artists. The six colors
of the flag, green, red, yellow, blue, white, and black,
became a frequently used color palette for the baskets, and the flag was represented on geometric as
well as on figurative baskets. Slogans such as "Bold
and Beautiful" appeared with the flag, and Nelson
Mandela's trips to Parliament and his wedding to
Graca Machel were honored by the weavers.

opposite page:
**ANC AND AFRICAN ART CENTRE OVAL PLATE**
Bheki Dlamini
320 x 340 mm
Campbell Collections, Durban

following pages, left:
**BOLD AND BEAUTIFUL**
Sibusiso Dhlodlo
260 mm diameter
Collection of Marianne Fassler

following pages, right:
**THE NEW SOUTH AFRICA**
Artist unknown
280 mm diameter
Collection of Marisa Fick-Jordaan

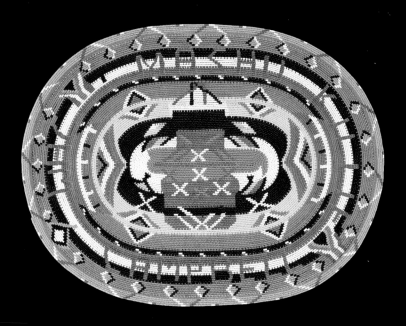

## WORDS

Many of the weavers started incorporating script in the early 1990s. The first basket that Elliot Mkhize sold to Paul Mikula included the artist's first name as a mark of his work. Bheki Dlamini and Dudu Cele took up the challenge of adding messages to embellish their baskets. Dudu focused on greeting-card messages; Bheki wove traditional Zulu titles such as Udwendwe Lukakoto (attendants in a traditional Zulu wedding) into his work.

top right:
**MERRY CHRISTMAS**
Dudu Cele
285 mm diameter
Collection of Marisa Fick-Jordaan

bottom right:
**KILLIE CAMPBELL PLATE**
Artist unknown
400 x 530 mm
Campbell Collections, Durban

opposite page, clockwise from top left:
**HAPPY YEAR 2001**
Bheki Dlamini
450 mm diameter
Collection of Marisa Fick-Jordaan

**BEWARE OF HIV AIDS**
Muriel Ntuli
410 mm diameter
Collection of Marisa Fick-Jordaan

**ONE TWO ONE**
Aron Ngobo
260 mm diameter
Collection of Marisa Fick-Jordaan

**BUS**
Bheki Dlamini
360 mm diameter
Collection of the Phansi Museum, Durban

## AIDS

AIDS has had a devastating effect on South Africa and particularly on the region of KwaZulu-Natal, which has the highest infection rate. In 2001 Durban hosted the thirteenth International AIDS Conference and, in support of this world event, the weavers created a whole series of AIDS baskets that were displayed at the Durban Art Gallery during the conference. Some of the most talented weavers, including Dudu Cele, have been lost to this pandemic.

opposite page:

**AIDS IS THE NUMBER ONE KILLER IN OUR PROVINCE**

Mboniseni Khanyile

395 mm diameter

Private Collection

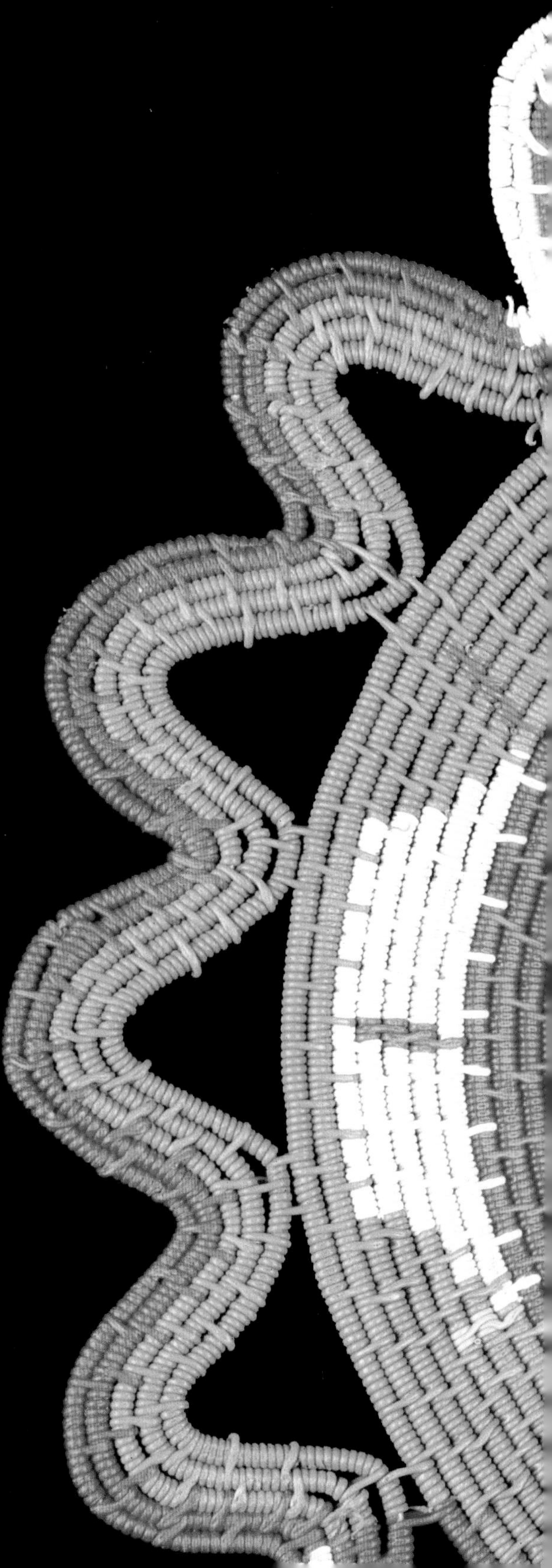

## FRILLY EDGES

The use of coiled wire as an edge or decorative detail was first introduced by Dudu Cele and later a more complex application of this innovation was developed by Rosalie Khanyile.

**MOTOR CAR**
Dudu Cele
270 mm diameter
Collection of Marisa Fick-Jordaan

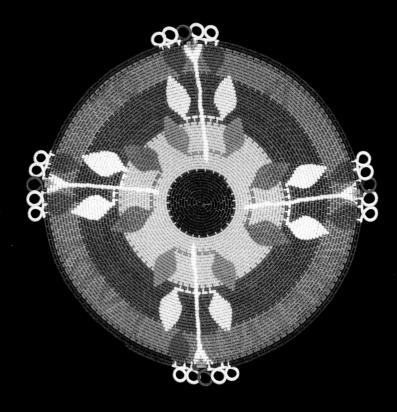

**TO A SPECIAL LADY**
Dudu Cele
280 mm diameter
Collection of Marisa Fick-Jordaan

**LOOPED FLOWERS**
Dudu Cele
240 mm diameter
Collection of Marisa Fick-Jordaan

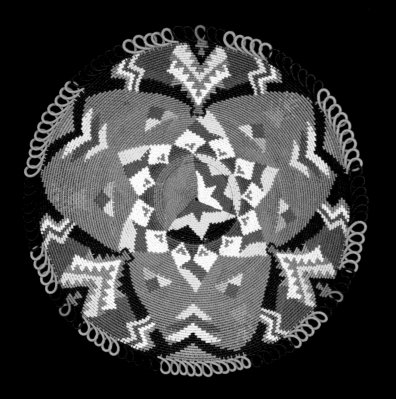

**PLATE WITH A LOOPED EDGE**
Artist unknown
355 mm diameter
Collection of Trisha Wilson

**PLATE WITH A FANCY EDGE**
Rosalie Khanyile
310 mm diameter
Collection of the Phansi Museum, Durban

## ARCHITECTURE

The incorporation of traditional Zulu huts and modern *rondavels* (a traditional round African house) started early on. Over time, details including doors and windows were added and images of larger structures such as the Parliament buildings and high rises are depicted; see, for example, the work of Bheki Dlamini and Dudu Cele. A commission from the Cape Town Tourism Association introduced Cape Dutch architecture. In his more recent large-scale works, Vincent Sithole clusters rows of huts to create the image of a traditional rural family settlement. Although most of the weavers have built their own urban homes in a square form, they continue to reference the more traditional *rondavel*, often playfully contrasting the colors of the walls and roofs.

opposite page:

### PLATE WITH HOUSE, JET, AND COW
Artist unknown
285 mm diameter
Collection of the Phansi Museum, Durban

following pages, left:

### CAPE DUTCH HOUSES
Zithobile Khambule
292 mm diameter
Private Collection

following pages, right, clockwise from top left:

### OVAL PLATE WITH HOUSES
Elliot Mkhize
390 x 320 mm
Private Collection

### SWIRLED PLATE WITH HUTS
Octavia Gwala
440 mm diameter
Collection of Marianne Fassler

### PLATE WITH FOUR HUTS
Nomthandazo Mtikitiki
286 mm diameter
Private Collection

### TURQUOISE HOUSES
Sylvia Mhlamvu
290 mm diameter
Private Collection

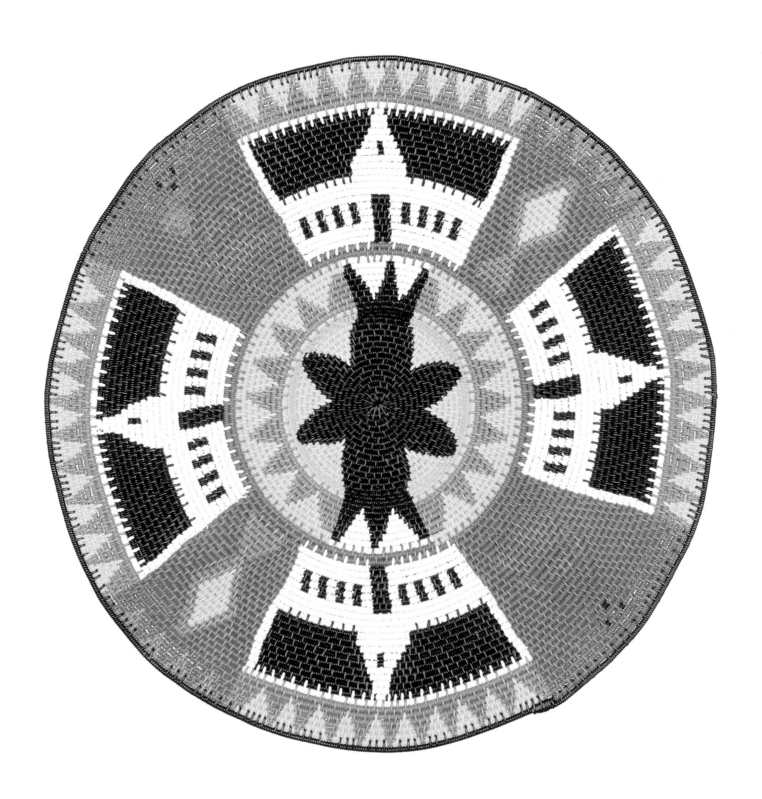

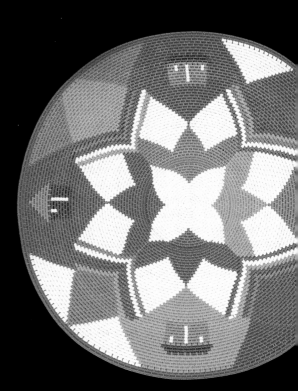

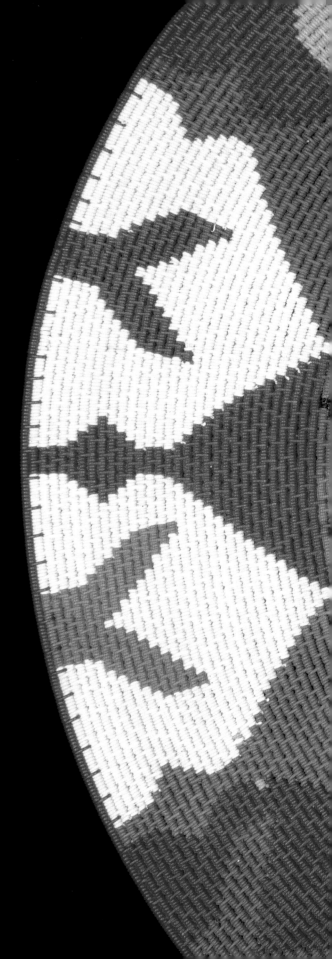

## ABSTRACTIONS

Geometric patterns, initially inspired by Zulu beadwork, particularly the complex patterns from the Nongoma district and those of Zulu earplugs from Msinga, have become more complex and more abstract as a result of suggestions and examples from other sources. The annual BAT calendars celebrating traditional Zulu artifacts became a major source of inspiration. Exhibitions showcasing the best examples of traditional Zulu material culture from private collections encouraged a renewed pride in local design. When the colors were available, traditional combinations were used, but later weavers began to experiment with a wider color palette as new colors were developed. With the emphasis placed on the development of individuality, increasingly sophisticated and intricate abstract geometric designs have emerged and the weavers are pushing the boundaries of traditional Zulu patterning.

**GEOMETRIC PLATE**
Nomthandazo Mtikitiki
370 mm diameter
Private Collection

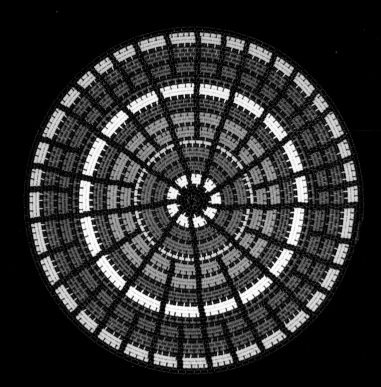

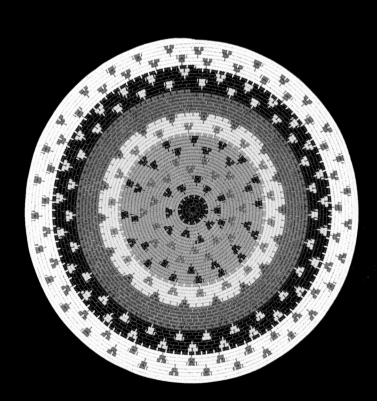

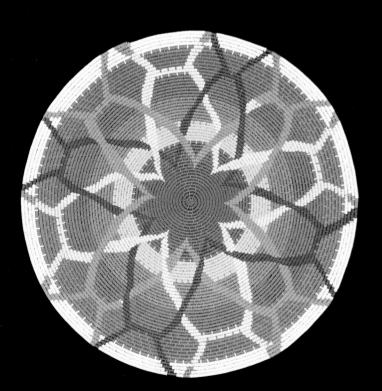

opposite page:

**ABSTRACT PLATE**

Khethayiphi Ndwandwe

273 mm diameter

Private Collection


previous pages, left, clockwise from top left:

**ABSTRACT PLATE**

Simon Mavundla

338 mm diameter

Private Collection

**ABSTRACT PLATE**

Joyce Mkhize

310 mm diameter

Private Collection

**ABSTRACT PLATE**

Joyce Mkhize

320 mm diameter

Private Collection

**ABSTRACT PLATE**

Joyce Mkhize

300 mm diameter

Collection of Margaret Daniel


previous pages, right, clockwise from top left:

**ABSTRACT PLATE**

Artist unknown

337 mm diameter

Private Collection

**ABSTRACT PLATE**

Nomthandazo Mtikitiki

335 mm diameter

Collection of Marisa Fick-Jordaan

**STAINED-GLASS PATTERN**

Vincent Sithole

318 mm diameter

Private Collection

**ABSTRACT PLATE**

Artist unknown

270 mm diameter

Collection of the Phansi Museum, Durban

## NATURE

Initially the weavers did not incorporate even common African wild animals; instead, they referenced domestic animals. And these, like the early human figures, were very simple, two-dimensional forms. Suggestions and examples persuaded the weavers to consider wild animals as possible elements of design; images of crocodiles and snakes, leopards, insects, rhinos, and so on have become used much more frequently. Many of the weavers now also incorporate a variety of plants, from commonly seen wild plants to wildly imaginative, multicolored trees.

**PLATE WITH GROUND HORNBILLS**
Dudu Celi
280 mm diameter
Collection of the Phansi Museum, Durban

**BLACK-AND-WHITE BOWL WITH FIGURES**
Alice Gcaba
120 x 380 mm
Collection of David Arment

**PLATE WITH TURTLE**
Solomon Nzimande
350 mm diameter
Private Collection

opposite page:
**TURQUOISE PLATE WITH FIGURES**
Florence Maquvana
457 mm diameter
Collection of David Arment

**PLATE WITH TREES WITH YELLOW FLOWERS**
Khethayiphi Ndwandwe
292 mm diameter
Private Collection

**CHAMELEON PLATE**
Vincent Sithole
337 mm diameter
Private Collection

opposite page:
**CHAMELEONS, BUGS, AND FLOWERS**
Vincent Sithole
540 mm diameter
Collection of Margaret Daniel

## BLACK AND WHITE

The weavers' inherent love of bright colors made them, initially, unreceptive to the possibility of producing monochromatic or even black-and-white baskets. The late Doris Mkhize and Bheki Dlamini were the first weavers to be persuaded, Doris creating a refreshing feather-and-arrow design radiating from a bold red dot in the center;  Bheki creating a dramatic dartboard design. Then Ntombifuthi Magwasa began playing with positive and negative patterns. Soon a repertoire of designs emerged that have become classics. Repetitions of popular designs became the first attempts at mass production and the results have led to a substantial business from international craft-marketing enterprises.

opposite page:
**GLASS BOTTLES COVERED IN**
**BLACK AND WHITE TELEPHONE WIRE**
Artists unknown
h: 305, 195, 315 mm
Private Collection

**BLACK-AND-WHITE PLATE WITH HUTS**
Sandile Nzimande
300 mm diameter
Private Collection

**BLACK-AND-WHITE PLATE WITH HUTS**
Sandile Nzimande
300 mm diameter
Private Collection

opposite page:
**BLACK-AND-WHITE PLATE**
Nombuso Nkwanyana
286 mm diameter
Private Collection

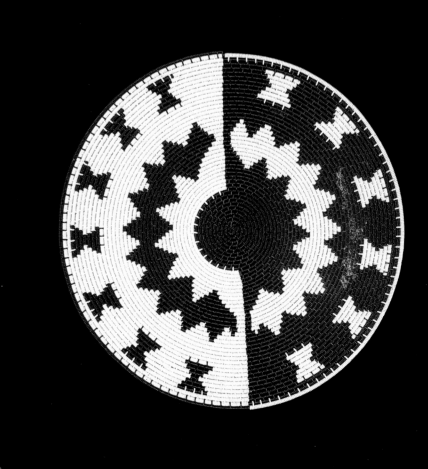

top left:
**BLACK-AND-WHITE PLATE**
Vusi Khanyile
273 mm diameter
Private Collection

bottom left:
**BLACK-AND-WHITE PLATE**
Phumelele Dumakude
318 mm diameter
Private Collection

opposite page, clockwise from top left:
**BLACK-AND-WHITE PLATE**
Artist unknown
215 mm diameter
Collection of Marisa Fick-Jordaan

**BLACK-AND-WHITE PLATE**
Khangi Mngadi
286 mm diameter
Private Collection

**BLACK-AND-WHITE PLATE**
Ntombifuthi Magwasa
250 mm diameter
Collection of Marisa Fick-Jordaan

**BLACK-AND-WHITE PLATE**
Sandile Nzimande
337 mm diameter
Private Collection

189

## ZENZULU

A commercial range of contemporary baskets, developed under the design direction of Marisa Fick-Jordaan, made by the weavers of Siyanda, and marketed under the trademarked name of zenzulu, is a fusion of contemporary design and the traditions of Zulu basket weaving. The range is being successfully marketed internationally, resulting in employment and development opportunities for the local community.

opposite page, clockwise from top left:

**RED ZENZULU LAMPSHADE BOWL**
380 mm diameter
Private Collection

**BLACK ZENZULU LAMPSHADE BOWL**
380 mm diameter
Private Collection

**RED WITH BLACK DOT ZENZULU LAMPSHADE BOWL**
380 mm diameter
Private Collection

**BLACK WITH RED DOT ZENZULU LAMPSHADE BOWL**
380 mm diameter
Private Collection

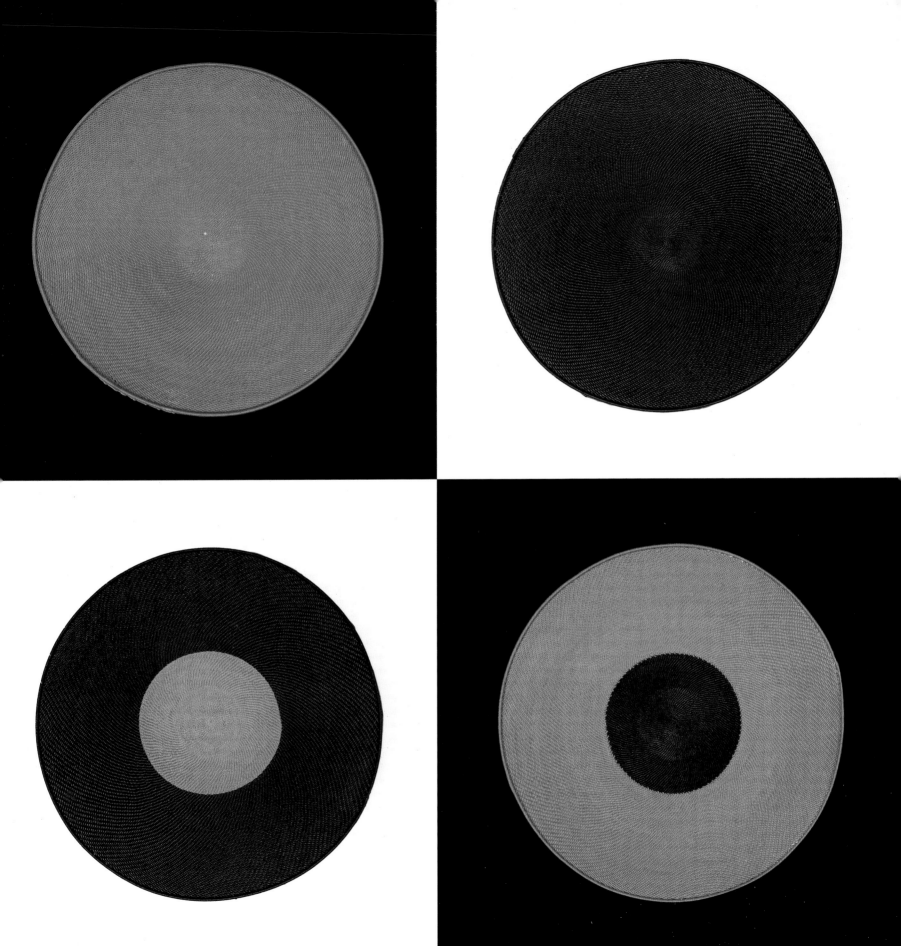

**AQUA SWIRL ZENZULU LAMPSHADE BOWL**
380 mm diameter
Private Collection

**TANGERINE-AND-PINK ZENZULU LAMPSHADE BOWL**
380 mm diameter
Private Collection

opposite page:
**LARGE BLACK-AND-RED VESSEL**
Jaheni Mkhize
275 x 350 mm
Private Collection

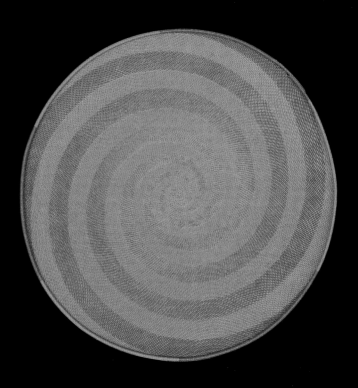

**BLACK ZENZULU LAMPSHADE BOWL WITH
THREE TELEPHONE-WIRE-COVERED OSTRICH EGGS**
Bowl 380 mm diameter, Eggs 140 x 180 mm
Private Collection

**FIVE LIME GREEN BOWLS WITH COPPER SWIRL, ZENZULU**
265, 222, 190, 152, 106 mm diameter
Private Collection

opposite page:
**THREE SPICE ZENZULU BOWLS**
200 x 180, 280 x 260, and 280 x 260 mm
Private Collection

**LIME ZENZULU LAMPSHADE BOWL**
380 mm diameter
Private Collection

**BLACK-AND-WHITE ZENZULU BOWL**
300 mm diameter
Private Collection

opposite page:
**FOUR POLKA-DOT BOWLS, ZENZULU**
180 x 160 mm
Private Collection

## UNDER PLATES

Once weavers mastered the ability to reproduce designs to a standard size, a flat tray with a rim was presented to the interior designer Boyd Ferguson, in the hope that he might find a use for it in the innovative Singita Lodge in the Sabi Sand Reserve, adjacent to the Kruger National Park in South Africa, that he was working on. Ferguson seized on the tray immediately and, since then, trays with different designs and colors have been developed for other lodges he has worked on. Because the guests kept asking for them, these under plates are also offered for sale in the boutiques attached to each lodge. They now grace tables around the world and ensure a steady income for a core of weavers.

opposite page, clockwise from top left:

**ZENZULU UNDER PLATE**
designed for the Lebombo Lodge
320 mm diameter
Private Collection

**ZENZULU UNDER PLATE**
designed for the Ebony Lodge
320 mm diameter
Private Collection

**ZENZULU UNDER PLATE**
designed for the Tsweni Lodge
320 mm diameter
Private Collection

**ZENZULU UNDER PLATE**
designed for the Boulders Lodge
320 mm diameter
Private Collection

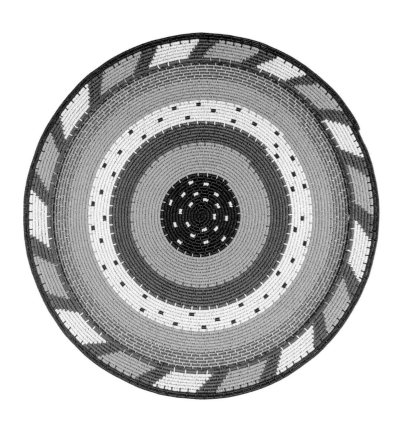

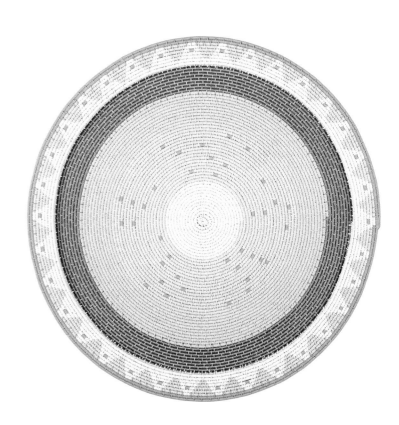

**TELEPHONE-WIRE BOWL WITH PORCUPINE QUILLS AND BEADS**
Artist unknown
130 x 330 mm
Collection of David Arment

**CERAMIC BOWL COVERED WITH TELEPHONE WIRE**
Joseph Msomi (wire) and Kim Sacks (ceramic)
100 x 140 mm
Private Collection

**ZENZULU FLUTED-RIM BOWL**
292 mm diameter
Private Collection

**COPPER WITH GLASS BEADS**
Artist unknown
216 mm diameter
Private Collection

## DIROZULU

The collaboration between the BAT Shop weavers and Hervé Di Rosa on mandalas for the Dirozulu project had a profound influence on the weavers' own work. The technical challenges presented by Di Rosa's figurative designs and their large scale presented some difficulties at first, but the weavers managed to overcome them. Vincent Sithole, in particular, has continued to use this flat format and has applied what he learned from Di Rosa into his own designs.

opposite page:
**EVOLUTION**
1999
Design by Hervé Di Rosa
Woven by Vincent Sithole
800 mm diameter
Private Collection
Photograph by Pierre Schwatrz

# GLOSSARY

**ABAFUNDUKI:** foreigners (Zulu)

**ABAFUNDISI:** teachers (Zulu)

**ABALUNGU:** white people (Zulu)

**AMADLOZI:** ancestors; ancestral spirits (Zulu)

**AMASUMPA:** a traditional decorative pattern used on Zulu clay pots

**AMATHWASA:** a trainee who is learning to become a traditional healer *(sangoma)*

**BAFANA BAFANA:** the Zulu name for the South African national soccer team

**BAT:** the Bartel Arts Trust, which funded the BAT Centre in Durban

**BAT CENTRE:** an arts-development center established by Bartel Arts Trust and located in Durban

**BAT SHOP:** an art and craft development and marketing enterprise located at the BAT Centre

**CETSHWAYO:** the monarch and ruler of the Zulu nation, who succeeded Shaka in the nineteenth century

**DURBAN STATION:** the original railway station in central Durban

**FNB VITA CRAFT NOW:** biannual craft awards sponsored by First National Bank

**HARD-WIRE WEAVING:** a coiled technique of weaving baskets, where telephone wire is coiled over a thicker base wire, typically made of aluminum

**HLABISA:** a rural district in northern KwaZulu-Natal

**IGOLI:** the city of Johannesburg, the largest in South Africa, a reflection of its gold production

**ILALA PALM:** an indigenous palm that grows mainly along the east coast of southern Africa and is traditionally used by the Zulu for weaving baskets

**IMBALI:** flower (Zulu)

**IMBENGE** (singular), **IZIMBENGE** (plural): a traditional Zulu beer-pot lid, the form that is the basis of contemporary Zulu telephone-wire plates and baskets

**ISISHUNKA:** an early Zulu beadwork pattern from the Msinga area

**ISITHEMBU:** an early Zulu beadwork pattern that came after the *isishunka*

**ISANDLWANA:** a famous battlefield; the site of a Zulu victory in 1879, during the Anglo-Zulu War

**JAHA:** to be in a hurry (Zulu)

**JABULISA:** a traveling exhibition of the art of KwaZulu-Natal, 1996, and a Zulu word for "to please"

**KAISER CHIEFS:** a well-known soccer team based in Johannesburg

**KIST:** a wooden storage chest

**KNOBKERRIES:** sticks used as weapons

**KWAMASHU:** a suburb of Durban, South Africa

**KWAZULU-NATAL:** a province of South Africa

**LOBOLA:** the traditional price for a bride in Zulu culture

**MASIBAMBANE TRUST:** a foundation established in 1994 by South African Breweries and Cosatu Affiliated Trade Unions to support economic development projects

**NDEBELE:** a northern Nguni tribe located in South Africa, the Ndebele people are well known for their artistic talent, especially with regard to their painted houses and colorful beadwork

**NGUNI:** a language group within southern Africa, the Nguni peoples are classified into three large subgroups: the Northern Nguni, the Southern Nguni, and the Ndebele, with the Zulu and the Swazi among the Northern Nguni

**NONGOMA:** a rural district in northern KwaZulu-Natal

**PHALAFINI:** a traditional Zulu beadwork pattern that came after the *umzansi*

**PORTNET:** the National Port Authority in South Africa

**RONDAVEL:** a traditional African house, a round structure with stone or mud walls covered by a thatched roof

**SCOOBIE WIRE:** colloquialism for PVC-coated copper telephone wire

**SHAKA:** a prominent nineteenth-century Zulu monarch

**SIYANDA:** an unincorporated settlement located outside Durban

**SOFT-WIRE WEAVING:** a technique of weaving, typically used for making bowls, without a base wire—instead the telephone wire is woven over a form, which is removed after the basket is completed

**TOG WORKER:** a casual laborer

**TAXIS:** privately run minibuses used as public transport in South Africa

**UDWENDWE LUKAKOTO:** attendants in a traditional Zulu wedding

**UKHAMBA** (singular); **IZINKHAMBA** (plural): traditional Zulu clay beer pot

**UMTHAKATHI:** to cast a bad spell or to bewitch

**UMSAMO:** a special place in the home set aside for conversation with the ancestors (domestic altar)

**UMVOTI:** a district of KwaZulu-Natal

**UMZANSI:** a traditional Zulu beadwork pattern that came after the *isithembu*

**USUNGULU:** a long needle used in Zulu basketry

**WAAYHOEK:** a resettlement community near Ladysmith developed for rural people who had been forcibly moved, by the apartheid regime, from areas designated for the exclusive use of whites, the Waayhoek project was one of the initial programs to build a commercial telephone wire basket market

opposite page:
**DETAILS OF TRADITIONAL WEAVING TECHNIQUES**
1. Typical basket construction, grass bundle spiral & *ilala* palm as binding
2. Detail of cable showing outer sheath and encased telephone wires
3. Plan of beginning of spiral, constructed with grass and palm
4. Grass spiral with telephone wire binding
5. Pattern making with grass and *ilala* palm using extended & dyed binding
6. Detail of spiral binding, showing how color stops and starts
7. Plan of beginning of spiral, constructed with galvanized wire and telephone wire
8. Galvanized wire spiral with telephone-wire binding
9. Detail of plaiting showing diagonal patterns generated by colored wires

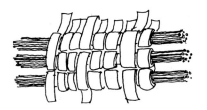

1

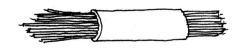

2

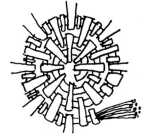

3

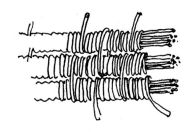

4

5

6

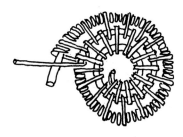

7

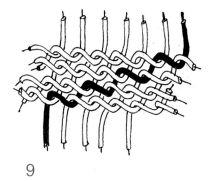

8

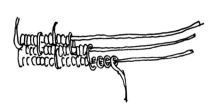

9